MANET

Jean-Jacques Lévêque

MANET

CRESCENT BOOKS
NEW YORK

Translated from the French by *Carol Lee Rathman*

This 1990 edition published by Crescent Books,
distributed by Crown Publishers, Inc., 225 Park Avenue South,
New York, New York 10003.

Printed and bound in Italy

ISBN 0-517-69479-4

h g f e d c b a

Table of contents

Index of illustrations

Manet's birthplace, Rue des Beaux-Arts.

Degas. *Portrait of Manet.*

Degas. *Manet at the Races.*

QUIET DAYS IN SAINT-GERMAIN DES PRES

Back then it was a quiet and solemn street – one of those that conferred a serene and at times melancholy air that smacked of provincialism in a Paris that was elsewhere marred by the vices and the ugly side of a commercially active city. It was a provincial street, inhabited by the bourgeoisie, lined with handsome and respectable residences (*hôtels*) occupied by a society steeped in piety, respect of institutions and venerability, and which drew strength from its habits and its formalities. It was also a little bit sleepy and resistant to (indeed, fearful of) any innovation or change, whether physical or intellectual, especially the latter, because ideas can do far more damage than deeds.

Faithful to the monarchy, this class sought to gain political control through it. It had put an Orléans in its own image on the throne, in opposition to a Bourbon, who represented an idea of power that it abhorred. The Bourbons derived a sense of superiority from the influence of very remote ancestors, while the bourgeoisie for the most part had risen up from the land, and it had taken generations of determination, hard work, self-sacrifice and ambitions to finally acquire a status of social responsibility, material comfort (albeit hard-earned) and prestige.

This class was parsimonious yet proud, mindful of appearances, yet wary of ostentation. Furthermore, whoever had struggled up the rungs of the social hierarchy was determined to not risk falling back down among the masses.

Though its members no longer had hayseeds in their hair, they retained the memory of that life, and feared it. They raised their children accordingly, so that there would be no chance of falling back to their origins. While the aristocracy played, the bourgeoisie made plans; while the scions of the great noble families consumed their lives in debauchery and vice, those of the new arrivals to the middle class consumed theirs in effort and work.

Any vague desire to deviate from this established course was brusquely dismissed by those who, by their example, their rigidity and their intransigence,

13

Study of a woman for *La Toilette*.
London, Courtauld Institute.

Après le Bain.
Paris, Louvre.

Women with Nude Breasts.
Paris, Louvre.

jealously protected their hard-earned interests, their honor and respectability, considered class and family assets.

For example, for a lawyer's son to take it into his head to become an artist was viewed as the most foolish whim, if not the most pernicious and dangerous choice. This was the case in the Manet family.

Edouard was to become a painter, but not before having gone through the mill of formal schooling. Though his was accepted as a true vocation, a calling, the bourgeois mentality insisted that a number of safety nets still be laid out.

Manet grew up in a quiet street, then, named "Petits Augustines" (today it is Rue Bonaparte) after the monastery erected nearby by Queen Margot, following numerous scandals over her outrageous misconduct. She was the Valois' favorite little sister, and Henri III's confidante. She was married to her Bourbon cousin, the Navarrian Henri IV. Repudiated, she ended her days in a residence under the protection of a religious order about which we have little information. Today there stands a magnificent chapel; in Manet's time there was a potpourri of architectural fragments set in what was the famous Jardin Elyséen, planned by Alexandre Lenoir, a picturesque and engaging character. Salvaging works of art that had fallen prey to revolutionist vandalism, their only crime having been that of testifying to the hated monarchy and aristocracy's existence, Lenoir had established a sort of lapidary museum whose charm owed as much to the setting as to the individual works of art.

Romanticism was born. Michelet imparted to it his passion for history and the love of his country. Manet came along too late to visit the paths winding among the tombs of heros who had fueled the dreams of Romanticism. This made him different, and gave his painting a different turn. The reality that he discovered was meatier and harsher, the reality of Paris waking up to modernity. Haussmann soon began his butchering of the city, ridding it of the pockets that still reflected its Medieval origins.

The bourgeoisie was proud of its money and power and the city planner's aim was to provide it with an opulent setting suited to these values, the same setting that Manet and his companions, the future Impressionists, would unveil as they revealed the world, its strengths and its glamour. And its weaknesses.

Manet's lawyer-father and his mother – a modest woman, though she was the god-daughter of King Bernadotte of Sweden – formed with their son a close-knit family steeped in traditional values. Manet's childhood unfolded untroubled in an atmosphere of luxury without ostentation, in a peace without fantasy, and colored with religion – it was the custom then to have the parish priest to dinner often.

The priest who frequented the Manet family was also Edouard's first teacher. Then the boy was sent to the faraway Vaugirard countryside, on the outskirts of Paris, where religious establishments had been set up to spread the holy Word. Incense, heavenly visions and leisurely walks through the gardens set the tone for the three years during which Manet got his introduction to culture. Subsequently he was sent to the Collège Rollin (near the Panthéon quarter of Paris), a stricter school, where nevertheless Manet already began to show his unique personality. He completed his general studies there, and despite his being a mediocre pupil, he was to be a very cultured man.

At school, even very early on, he showed off his talent for drawing. More than once, he was caught covering the pages of his notebook with sketches instead of Latin declentions. Enough evidence still remains to stoke the fires of legend today. Manet had a prolific hand. And when he was allowed to take special courses in drawing, he persisted in sketching his classmates rather than carrying out such assignments as representing "Henri III's Entry into the Good City of Paris".

Manet was not to be a historical painter.

Destined by the logic of his social class to a career

in law, Manet rebelled against his father's wishes. In this, he was a generation ahead of his time, which made him a favorite target of the period's chroniclers. Though he was not spared his share of doubts, he was possessed by a determination typical of great vocations.

His law career on the rocks, he embarked on a career at sea. The artist himself decided on this course, seconded by his father who had gradually been forced by his son's obstinacy to renounce his initial ambitions. When Manet failed to pass the Naval school entrance examination the only remedy was to enter in active service. He accepted this turn of events unflinchingly, and so the young member of the bourgeoisie, already distinguished and refined in his manners, met head on with a group of rough seamen, whose rudeness did justice to the legend.

On December 9, 1848, Manet boarded ship at Le Havre, his destination Rio de Janeiro. He returned from this adventure in June 1849. Having again failed the entrance examinations, his plans for this future were definitively broken off. If he could not be a sailor, then he would turn to painting the sea. In his brief career as a seaman, he had come to know the sea very well, he had haunted it and its port towns. But he would not make a myth of it; he was just a city dweller who had strayed to the ocean. He was to stray into the world of painting and there seek his harbor.

Aboard ship, he had taken advantage of his abundant free time to keep up his habit of drawing what was around him. He sketched his shipmates and had not lost his gift. His eye was trained. What remained for him was to channel his creative energies.

His father conceded. Edouard was to be a painter.

Thus, Manet selected his master: Thomas Couture, who had become famous for one painting. It had been the main attraction at the 1847 Salon. Entitled *The Romans of the Decadent Period*, it was one of the most successful examples of a trend in art which focused more on the subject matter than on technique, continuing the academicism of David, but distorting his fundamental purity, his conceptual rigor. It is noteworthy that in conforming to the fashion for subjects from the pages of ancient history, Couture had selected one illustrating debauchery.

Beyond the glitter and polish of "good" art technique, jealously defended by the official artists (the "pompiers", stuffed shirts), lay the weakness and the nightmares of a society that before long criticized Manet for openly expressing its own most shameful thoughts. The language of feelings sought its author, and Manet was ready to step into that role.

Choirboy.
Private collection.

Portrait of Baudelaire.

Photograph of Baudelaire.

They were made to meet one another. And to admire each other. The elegance of a dandy, the style of a prince, a touch of haughtiness, and of eccentricity were all qualities that the two men shared. We have a portrait of Baudelaire from this period. It was the frontispiece of Michel Lévy's publication (1868): "His face is expressionless and clean-shaven, his hair short; he is dressed in a very roomy sort of jacket, elegantly styled, with a loose tie knotted with studied insouciance around a broad, barely starched collar, turned down to expose his neck" (François Porché, *Baudelaire*, Editions Plon).

The Goncourts were immediately stricken by his physical fascination, describing it as the "true bearing of a man condemned to the guillotine". This was the fatalist and tragic aspect of the poet. His pride hid a deep anxiety that blossomed into *Les Fleurs du Mal*, published in 1857 by Malassis. Written with fervor and patience, the product of several years' intense work and fruitful disregard, this book was dedicated "in a solemn and terse way" (François Porché, *Baudelaire*, Editions Plon) to Théophile Gautier. It fell victim to the pen of a scurrilous hack writer at the service of narrow-minded morals who denounced it as a book in which "the odious rubs shoulders with the ignoble, and rejecting even that, strikes up an alliance with the vile".

A statement of this kind published in a journal whose function it was to uphold the ruling political forces, could only have one outcome: legal prosecution.

The poet's supporters could not hold in check the mounting wave of hostility against this book and its author. A coalition was formed that succeeded in prohibiting even the publication of articles in his favor, such as the one written by Barbey d'Aurevilly.

The scandal did ensure the book's success, but the poet was fined 300 francs. What was worse was that his crime was realism.

Before long Manet would experience the same black hole of scandal and incomprehension.

They met at one of those soirées that they both were so fond of attending, perhaps Baudelaire even more than Manet. One final point of communion between the two men was that their familial situations were similar.

Manet's life was torn between his parents' severity as they anxiously watched over his disorderly existence as a painter, and an almost clandestine ménage where he lived in Les Batignolles, with a mistress and son kept well in the background.

Baudelaire had a relationship with Jeanne Duval which had been drawn out way past its time. She was "old, ugly, ill, stupid, mean, dishonest, perverse, besotted with drink, but after all, she is Jeanne." This was all that remained of the black Venus whom Baudelaire had met when she was acting in a small part at the Théatre du Panthéon. He had been wandering from hotel backroom to hotel backroom. So, in a moment of weakness, he wrote, "I must at all costs take a family. I shall start a relationship".

He had just gotten back from Honfleur, having fled there from an old mistress and a new home in the Bastille quarter (22 Rue Beautreillis), where Jeanne also lived, alone. Equally alone, Baudelaire preferred the anonymity of hotel life, and selected one in the Saint-Lazare neighborhood, Hôtel du Dieppe, Rue d'Amsterdam.

He was alone and wounded, proud and pitiful when he met the very young artist Manet, whom he admired from the very start. Manet was just at the beginning of his career, and eleven years separated them.

Baudelaire immediately sensed a kindred soul in this man. Manet was anxious to know his reactions to a painting, *The Absinthe Drinker*, which had been harshly criticized by his master Couture, among others. Manet had painted it during the winter of 1858-59, having taken as his subject a well-known clochard who haunted the Pigalle neighborhood. This model's name was Collardet, and he was well known for having poured all of his genius into drink. To have painted a drunkard's mug showed a break with the then-current trend of painting History. The art establishment painted illusions while he had sought Reality, whether unpleasant, depressing, hateful or ugly.

Paradoxically, Baudelaire, carver of the most perfect verbal gems, loved the subject and understood the allusion, but he was somewhat reserved about the technique. It still reflected academicism, formulas, the master's atelier, for all that it suggested modernity and the promise of "a painter, a true painter, who would make us see and understand how great and poetic we are, with our ties and patent leather boots". Manet was still too insecure and embarrassed by the weighty heritage of academicism. But perhaps modernity was meant to tear down the stage props, to express the street and its poverty, to let them have their say in the shadow of a society that was so hung up on its dignity; it meant telling the truth about life. Manet carried the banner of modernity in the name of this truth.

Absinthe Drinker.
Copenhagen, Carlsberg Glyptothek.

Still Life with Fish and Oysters.
Chicago, Art Institute.

Boy Blowing a Soap Bubble.
Fundação Calouste Gulbenkian.

24

The Tuileries had always been a place for the common people, despite its proximity to the king's palace. Painted by Manet in its definitive version, this park had been witness to moments of both glory and tragedy. Under the Second Empire, it had become a center of Parisian life. The place became fashionable, enhanced by the aura of splendor surrounding the court life in the Tuileries palace. Certain customs developed. The Emperor kept an English-style garden for his exclusive private use (where the Rue Paul Déroulède presently passes), leaving to the common people the shady walks and magnificent stretch of greenery that was the Champs Elysées.

Between the Tuileries and the Champs Elysées there was a constant flow of life – of the sort that set fashions but which Manet had already foreshadowed in his drawings. An effect of depth was created to please his royal majesty. It became a playground for pleasure to gratify the naughty whims and sensuality of an epoch that marched to this tune. The bourgeoisie of the Third Republic inherited the style and ways of life of the Second Empire and the Tuileries was the favored location of its worldly promenade.

Manet's choice of the Tuileries as the setting for the characters of his world was echoed by Proust in his *Récherche du Temps Perdu*. The writer had strolled through the copses of the nearby Champs Elysées to gather the emotions that blossomed into his perception of the world. At the two ends of this park, then, one world perished under the weight of pictorial modernity, and another was born of the irrepressible surge of sensations that were to become the subject themselves of all creative activity that followed.

It is fitting that the old clichés of art were finally extinguished in a park. Manet shook off the last constraints of this art as he sounded out the future.

The park was a world in itself, inhabited by people who could hardly distinguish one another in the blaze of colors and the dancing play of light, this

House at Rueil.
Berlin, Staatliche Museum.

Head of Woman.
Private collection.

The Convalescent.
Paris, Louvre.

abrupt alternation of black and white. The rustling of silk, the whisper of organdies, the rippling nonchalance of ribbons, the heavy smoothness of elegantly styled men's jackets, the shadowplay of opera hats, pools of light stopped by parasols: Manet offered a symphony, a shimmering of colors and sensations wherever he stopped to do a portrait of an elegant group.

It was still a far cry from the sensuality of Renoir's *Moulin de la Galette*, composed and orchestrated in 1876, where workers in their Sunday best roosting nonchalantly on heavy kitchen chairs, and florid, overly-painted girls (no doubt dressmakers' apprentices, barmaids or house servants and governesses) gathered around the park benches.

Manet's world was whirling and frivolous, stiffened only by its dignity. Manet respected the hieratic order, but he managed to break through it and interrupt its rhythm with his uneven lines and a frontal perspective that may even seem clumsy. He intentionally set in the foreground a disordered array of scrolled metal chairs, open parasols resting on the ground, and children at play, transforming what otherwise could not have been anything but a cold and stilted display, into the space of expectation, a pose, an interlude.

In fact, there are no musicians in sight, despite the title that announces them: *Musiques aux Tuileries*. Manet decided to turn his back on the source of the spectacle, in order to make a spectacle of the spectators themselves. This was the skilful and meaningful about-face of the painter-turned-voyeur, chronicler of his times, of his society. He did not indulge in useless details; it was the whole that interested him, the effect of the mass. Nevertheless, he included his friends and accomplices: Baffroy appears, along with Théophile Gautier, Lord Taylor, Champfleury, Lesjone, Fantin-Latour (who returned the compliment in his *Atelier aux Batignolles*), and even Baudelaire. It was a group portrait, a sort of worldly map where luxury and reality, a fascination for society and for nature, a

conspiratory tenderness and a ruthless lucidity all came to clash. It goes beyond the chronicle, to the exhileration of a painting that expresses sensations. In the same way, Proust, describing the same world with equal unforgiveness, went beyond the account into a very new and exhilerating world of special sensations, which was to be the subject and vehicle from here on in of a great many works.

AT THE RISK OF BECOMING AN OFFICIAL ARTIST

Georges Bataille assures us that Manet was not imaginative, pointing out that "he studied through the night, plagued with doubts, to find a solution to the decay of the old style of art". This was the most intimate side of the man, buried under the appearance of a disconcerting ease, and pride which he willingly exhibited (but no doubt to hide his weaknesses). Again, his elegance in attire was just another way of better camouflaging his worn nerves, the devastating consequence of his painting.

His early works were marked by a searching, tentative quality whose only certainty was a furious passion for all that was Spanish.

It is as if Manet turned to Vélasquez for redemption from life as a "pompier" – an official artist – just another "stuffed shirt" in a period in which they abounded, swaggering and titillating the sensibilities of the bourgeois class. He was distressed by this era, in which it was better to flaunt the most impudent self-assurance. Doubt was a luxury that he could ill afford in a social structure that had such fragile foundations, and whose only comfort lay in its money and the hope of more of it by playing the card of industry, daughter of trade and technology. The only hope for gratification.

It was paradoxical that a society so open to technological progress should be so closed to the evolution of thought. It fiercely clung to the conventions that had held it together as it was ostensibly making its transition to an industrial economy, the source of all conflict and a destroyer of tradition. It is also paradoxical that Baudelaire, bard of modernity in painting, should feel nothing for this world to come but an "immense bewilderment". He spoke of the "great industrial madness that was putting an end to the bliss of dreaming".

The poet was intoxicated with the twilight passions of Delacroix and harbored great misunderstandings about Manet, calling him a genius of truth. He confused truth with the picturesque phase Manet was passing through, for lack of having within himself his own path and subjects, in his "Spanish" period.

The Spanish Singer.
Private collection.

Victorine Meurent in Espada Costume.
New York, Metropolitan Museum.

Fisherman.
Private collection.

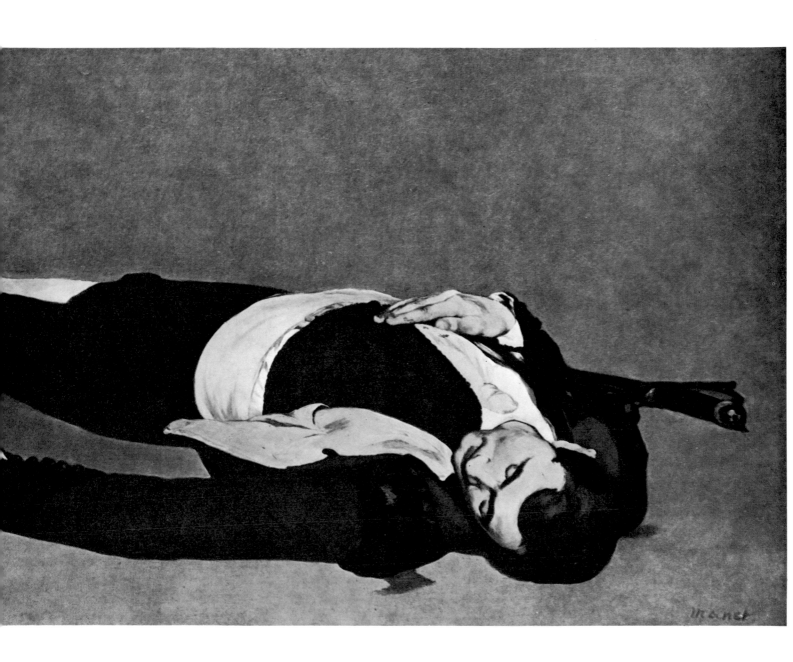

He made Lola de Valence into a symbol for his admiration, calling it "the unexpected charm of a pink and black jewel".

Baudelaire was at the limit of his painful egotism and on the brink of the abyss of a desperate and total solitude. Manet, dazzled by the glittery trimmings of an art that, however, gave rise only to conventional and banal subjects. He was still far from the reality that awaited him. Baudelaire applauded his boldness, which did not lie in his subject matter but in his style. Moreover the poet's applause was for a style that was still conditioned by the ateliers and museum examples, and by the artist's admiration for Vélasquez.

Nevertheless, Manet's hispanomania led him to a few pictorial results that played greatly in his favor. His indubitable talent as a painter was widely and generously recognized around him. Finally, admission to the Salon was the icing on the cake.

It was with the *Spanish Singer* (also called *The Guitarerro*) that he took this big step.

A popular Andalusian guitarist, Huerta, offered Manet the inspiration for this painting. The artist knew a sort of tramp who had the look he was seeking, and invited him to the studio in Rue de Donai to pose. He placed a guitar in the tramp's hands, committing the error of depicting him as left-handed (for a champion of naturalism and truth in painting this was a shortcoming). But the painting lost none of its brilliance for this inexactitude, and the subject none of its charm. Théophile Gautier (who was gaining recognition as an authority in painting) was enthusiastic about it and wrote, "Caramba. This is a guitarerro who has not stepped out of the Opéra Comique and who would not look good as a romantic novel illustration. But Vélasquez would have given him a friendly wink and Goya would have asked him for a match to light his *papelito*".

Apart from his extravagant turns of phrase and his bobs to anecdote for the purpose of seducing his readers, Gautier stated the essential.

Manet had managed to go directly to the heart of Spain, not so much through his subject matter, but through his style which reflected a disillusioned magnificence, a calm luxuriance with an obscure foreboding of disaster underlying the procession of images. Since he looked at Spain from without, Manet did not achieve this effect by depicting the country's tinselly folklore (though this is what the public begged for to lift them out of their state of torpor, and to prod them out of their shells in quest of an unusual color that they could not find within their familiar surroundings) – he offered that special quickening of the soul that happens only in crucial moments to strayed spirits. He penetrated beyond the fire and flamboyance of street music, to the disillusion of who is playing it. Though he was short on imagination, Manet made up for this with his ardent sensibilities. His street singer commanded the attention of a jury known for its severity. Ingres was part of it, but as was his habit, did not participate in the deliberations, nor did Delacroix and Horace Vernet. Other artists, completely forgotten today, laid down the law: Abel de Pujol, Schnetz and Couder among others. He also drew the prickly and intolerant attention of Heim, Picot, Bracassat, Alaux and Signol, as well as the more moderate understanding of Cogniet, Robert Fleury and Flandrin. It may have been the relative liberalism of the latter that determined Manet's admission to the Salon. Or it may have been his presentation, alongside the *Street Singer*, of the double portrait of his parents. This portrait contained none of the Spanish qualities of the other, and very simply and economically conveyed that sort of pinched gravity of the bourgeoisie through two of its most typical representatives.

At the unveiling of the portrait, Manet's parents came to admire the framed version of themselves as well as to see their celebrated son applauded by his peers. On this occasion they met Baudelaire, whom Manet had never had the courage to bring to any of his mother's tea parties.

Madame Sabatier, dubbed by her friends "the President", was noted among the stylish and exclusive attending public.

Her friends – that is, habitués of her Salon in Rue Frochot – included Musset, Flaubert, Sainte-Beuve, the Goncourts, Barbey d'Aurevilly, Gautier, Feydeau, Maxime du Camp, Meissonier, Clésinger and Baudelaire, who in a strange and clandestine way was in love with her. For five years he had sent her anonymous messages and rhymed verse, disguising his handwriting.

Another woman present attracted much attention: Princess de Metternich, who ensured the worldly success of any event she attended, because she only went where it was in her best interest to be seen, so that later she could say that she had been there – and her saying this to the Court guaranteed a significant portion of high society visitors that could not be overlooked.

Manet basked in the exhibition's success, confirmed by such illustrious presences, and he felt in top form. Even his father was impressed by this. He saw in this worldly effervescence the best guarantee of a brilliant career. No doubt the Manet who had been accepted by his peers, smug, self-indulgent academicians and painters, was a transitory character still in search of himself. When he finally did find himself, he was lost to this group.

After the song, there is the dance: Spain again, this time dressed as a woman. Manet met her at the Hippodrôme.

Never had the Champs Elysées reflected so well its mythological name as on these summer evenings that seemed to penetrate the darkness on a trail of perfumes, and women, glittering reflections that colored the night in a seductive and intoxicating aura. It stunned the curious onlookers who were reluctant to abandon their enjoyment of the instant, this calm majesty of nature dressed for a party, nature in its seasonal glory. They gathered round the slightest incident, the most insignificant sight. Huge crowds gathered, immobile at the same time flowing. Manet

was there, slow in his movements and as if sleepwalking. He was a member of the bourgeoisie among others of his kind. With an elegant and nonchalant air, he was ready for all the stimulation that the time and place could offer him, where the lady-flowers made it all worth while; love was at the top of the program, beneath the barely rustling foliage of the finest park that Paris had to offer at the time.

Pleasant places to sip a drink and to observe abounded in the most hidden corners of the park. The light of the street lamps, strings of lights, the eye-catching and enticing signs danced. Spectacle was king here.

Preceded by its brilliant reputation, a Spanish dance troupe offered a show at the Hippodrôme. Manet went there attracted like many others by the passion of the music and the blare of the colors. Thus he met Lola de Valence. She was a proud and passionate woman, not one of the most beautiful, but one of the boldest. She burnt up the stage in a concert of strange, throaty, gutteral moans accompanied with nervous, imperious, jerky steps that struck to the hearts of the spectators. She had a physical hold over her public, so lively was her sensuality and so strong her appeal. Manet too was drawn to this and he felt compelled to set its strange beauty on canvas. In fact, two paintings were born of it: a group scene and a standing portrait of the lead female dancer. For the latter, he had the dancer pose for him in the studio made available to him by an elegant man of the world, Alfred Stevens, in 18 Rue de Taitbout.

Lola de Valence, the queen of warm Parisian nights, was on stage as she was in Manet's painting, dressed in pink and vermillion. She wore her hair like a gypsy, with a tortoiseshell comb holding a mantilla in place over her head; her eyebrows were thick, her lashes smeared with kohl and her eyelids heavy, shaded in blue to emphasize their depth and fire.

By Manet's side in this discovery and the adventure in painting that followed was Baudelaire, who

41

composed the poem that reflected in words the message of the image: "Entre tant de beauté que partout on peut voir/je comprends bien que le désir balance/mais on voit dans Lola de Valence/le charme d'un bijou rose e noir."

Manet-Baudelaire under the light of Spain: this could have been a happy ending for a gifted painter in good company who had long searched for his true self. He seemed to have found it. This is well known, but it reflects a poor knowledge of the painter and his time. He was not frivolous, but his time was.

It was not long before the painter, who already had an adulating public, was held in contempt. Just a few tactless remarks from a critic about the man and his genre were enough to tumble him into the inferno of misunderstanding.

An entire series of Spanish works, with Victorine Meurent appearing in the guise of a bullfighter, was yet to come. But it was especially in the wake of the *Olympia* scandal of the 1865 Salon (where, according to Paul de Saint Victor, "the crowd pressed as if at the morgue before the tainted Olympia) that Manet felt he had to escape Paris, where his budding genius was stifled and cramped, moving in silent revolt against injustice and incomprehension. Revolt was neither in his character nor in his habits. He fled to Spain so that his art could share in, according to what he had heard, the spirit of that majestic "school". He went to the source. He was disappointed, not by the art he found there – it was like his own – but rather by the country itself, which he had believed to be permeated with a romanticism that once there eluded him. To the contrary, he found it to be wretchedly picturesque.

Lastly, what he had admired in the Spanish painters was not so much their style (which he had achieved on his own, quite alone) as their particular vision of reality which could be interpreted as intensity.

The excess of vitality juxtaposed so pathetically with the concept of death, an exaggerated form of worship, brought Manet to the conclusion that he too had subjects from reality whose intensity lay in their modernity.

We shall return to this. For him, it was inevitable. Thus, Baudelaire had seen him for what he was, or rather what he was to become: the bard of his time.

To say that he found in Spain the painting style that he had been seeking would be false. It would be more correct to say that he was rediscovering it, since he had already achieved it. What he did find there was the reality that until then had escaped him.

In his Spanish period, one work sprang from an idea that is a good example of the innovation that was so poorly received in its time.

Paradoxically, it was an incomplete work that narrowly escaped destruction at the hands of the painter, so angry and disappointed was he over the negative reaction it aroused at the 1864 Salon.

It started as a painting entitled *Episode in a Bullfight.*

Working in his studio, he took his hispanic fantasies to an extreme, a sort of tragic echo of his *Posada*, executed in about the same period in Alfred Stevens' studio in Rue Taitbout.

Not very satisfied with the painting, Manet did the unwise thing of presenting it at the 1864 Salon. Humorists set the tone by stating, "These are Spanish toys prepared with a black Ribera sauce by Monsieur Manet y Courbetaos y Zurbaran de las Batignolles".

This jibe contained an accurate identification of Manet's references: the crude realism of Courbet and the sobriety of Zurbaran contributed to it's; spiritual dimension, which arises from the most ordinary reality and the grandeur that speaks of a man engaged in a basic struggle. Dividing the canvas into two parts, the *Bullfight* and *The Dead Torero*, Manet created a masterpiece. Extended for the length of the canvas and seen from a diagonal perspective that emphasizes the stiffness of the corpse and its heavy immobility, the dead torero is set against a red and black background that is extraordinary for the unity of the two colors which merge, deforming the space and resulting in an almost abstractly simple color-space occupied by death alone.

The Spanish reference in this painting takes the form of a toreador, though any other of our mythical figures would have done as well. Spain was a recurrent motif in Manet's work and imagination. What is more important is that the painting depicts a dead man dressed for a procession in which he takes the role of victim. It is a dramatized, faked death that reaches beyond the immediate spectacle, arriving at a sort of dignity, though also at the frightening and inexorable finality of solitude.

The spectators are no longer there to justify the spectacle, nor the accomplices, the other players in an act of which nothing remains but a victim spread out under the sun, seen from a lively photographic angle, like a vulgar news item covered by the gutter press. Manet, having gotten to that point, having anticipated it, galvanized it with a pictorial handling free of flashy effects or sensational details, imbuing it with a sort of dignity that offers its subject a rare beauty and a unique grandeur.

What was modern about this painting was that it was about the greatest disaster that could befall man, one which haunts him: death.

His contemporaries turned away from him. To speak so nudely of death, without resorting to the usual anecdotal sugar-coating in such a dark, objective, natural way, seemed the worst sort of indecency.

The growth of Paris and the lasting modifications of its urban fabric caused its centers of activity to shift locations. Economic factors related to this led to the isolation of artistic life.

For as long as the artist was an integral part of the monarchic power structure, his master and sovereign provided lodgings for him in the space in the Louvre palace left free by the Court's transferral to Versailles. A sort of community was established in the Grande Galerie that lasted for several generations of artists. But the painter remained highly dependent on his primary patron. The disintegration of these structures and the considerable changes in the definition of the artist in a social context that no longer offered him a functional role led to the dispersal of living quarters and studios. The atmosphere of intimacy and exchange between artists that had been created at the Louvre found a natural new home in the cafés, so that by the close of the 19th century they were centers of information and battle. The cafés provided the arms and from them were launched the bombs that rocked the established order and the heritage of the past.

Rather than explode, the artistic milieu followed the laws of urban growth. Renewal zones and spaces destined to new construction were created, leading to an appreciable increase in the cost of living. Thus, artists' studios progressively drifted toward non-urbanized areas, abandoned by those who had felt the urge to move to the city.

Les Batignolles was one such place. A village that had been absorbed by Paris, it had preserved its character as a village and offered low cost living spaces.

To the contrary, the nearby town of Monceau underwent rapid urbanization. Elegant, it attracted the nouveaux riches who had benefited by the burgeoning economies of the Second Empire and the Third Republic. It was a residential quarter, but fashionable and even prestigious. It was considered elegant. On the Rive Droite, it was a counterpart to the venerable and very old suburb of Saint-

Germain, occupied by the old aristocracy which, though ruined by the Revolutions, had clung to its customs, its breeding, family ties, clan spirit and parochialism.

The inhabitants of the Monceau plain were infinitely more open, extravagant and inclined to burn their candles at both ends to make their recent rise in society seem credible.

It was only natural that artists celebrated by a society that included the families of the artists themselves should settle in the Monceau neighborhood, and that innovative artists who had been rejected by the bourgeoisie – and who would soon be led to oppose vigorously this class, prejudices, whether social or cultural – should settle in the immediately neighboring area of Les Batignolles, which had not lost its provincial character.

Tired of nymphs paddling about in stage-set rivers and of tawdry Olympias at their baths, Manet dreamed of a real woman, true-to-life. He rejected Ingres' odalisques, though the old master's sensuality had endowed them with a quality that would haunt Degas in his search for a natural woman with a touch of the sinful about her.

Manet wished to paint a woman who was of his own time, offering no finery other than her own beauty, a beauty however that was not dictated by fashion. Even nudity was subject to the whims af fashion. What he sought was such a candid realism that it could transcend the centuries and speak of ordinary women, of the essence of womanhood and not just their bodies: the total woman and not just the studio model. He imagined an instant, if not an action, which called for the presence of the servant and the splendid bouquet of flowers to act as the "decorative" counterpoint to the lascivious pose of a woman on her couch.

Directness was what armed his vision. A friend of Baudelaire's and a faithful reader of his ardent, scintillating poetry, Manet tinged his scene with that obscure and disturbing aura that Baudelaire attributed to cursed femininity. Manet's *Olympia* contained an implicit homage to *Les Fleurs du Mal*. The elastic, supple presence of the cat in the painting was the link with Baudelaire's world, full of odors, caresses, spasms and a splendid but neurotic voluptuousness.

No one could have served Manet as a model better than Victorine Meurent, in a work into which he poured so much of himself and his paradoxical style, as marked by the crudest, truest and clearest realism as it was by the most sophisticated fiction, destroyer of common habits of seeing and conceiving the world.

The public was disturbed both by the apparent realism of the female presence and by something which eluded it, that margin of sensuality that Manet owed to Baudelaire.

At once spontaneous and labored, rapid in his sketches and painstaking in his final versions,

Still Life with Peonies.
Paris, Louvre.

Sketch for *Olympia.*
Private collection.

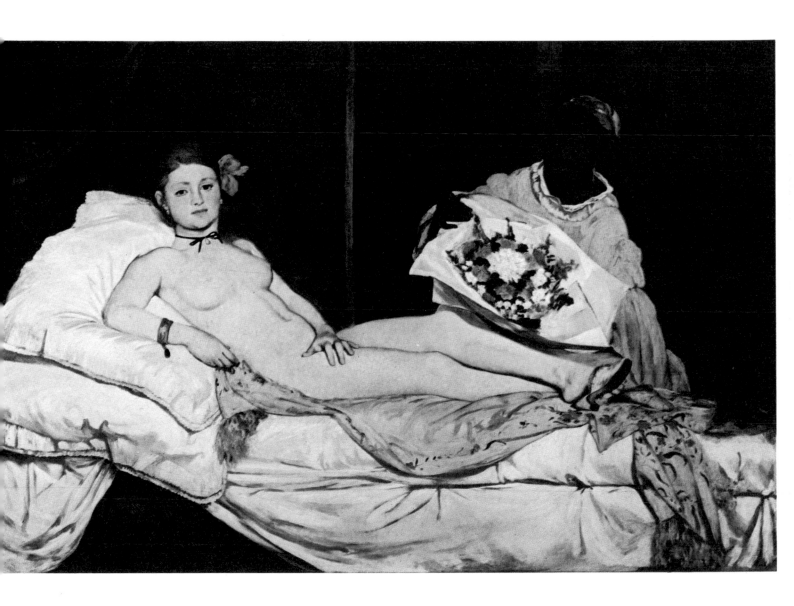

Manet painted just an impression of the reclining woman, the cat, the servant with her bouquet. He had the stage set, the characters and the objects. What remained was to make this vision of fire, passion and unconscious morbidity tangible.

He had Victorine pose. At first it was a painting without a title. Zacharie Astruc hit upon one, *Olympia*, and for this "child of the isles" (Baudelaire was decidedly in the wings here) he composed a long erotic exotic poem, an extract of which was presented alongside the painting at the Salon.

"Quand lasse de rêver, Olympia s'éveille
"le printemps entre au bras du doux messager noir;
"C'est l'esclave, à la nuit amoureuse pareille,
"qui vient fleurir le jour délicieux à voir
"l'auguste jeune fille en qui la flamme veille."

This created an aura of sensuality about the painting that the public perceived as an insult.

The Salon of 1865 flirted with tolerance and opened its doors wide (3,559 admissions), but Manet's presentation was almost unanimously met with jeers and criticism.

People went to see *Olympia* as if it were a circus attraction, to deride it.

So much negative publicity from the start was only exacerbated on sight of the work, which had been well calculated to irritate immature minds, tangled in their webs of prejudices, prudishness and ill will towards anything that could disturb their habitual way of thinking and seeing. The woman was found to be ugly. And lewd.

"Who is this yellowish-bellied odalisk, ignoble model picked up heaven knows where," wrote Jules Claretie, adding, "We are not reproaching Monsieur Manet for having idealized mad virgins. It is just that they are sullied virgins."

"An unthinkable vulgarity," commented further Ernest Chesneau.

Strangely, the *Olympia* was met with laughter. "There are nuggets of gaity hidden in the figure's modeling and in the lines of the whole (...)" or again,

"Monsieur Manet will not hold it against us if we burst into laughter at the sight of his *Olympia*".

Underlying the scorn was the fear that Manet's art would gain acceptance. Judith-Théophile Gautier deminstrated extraordinary insight when she wrote the straightforward and prophetic remark that "the exhibition has its buffoon... Among all the artists, he is a man who has taken to turning somersaults and to sticking out his tongue, but there is nevertheless something to be feared. Monsieur Manet could well gain acceptance."

Critics found the *Olympia* to be decadent, and comparing it to a bearded lady, feared that upon seeing it pregnant women and young girls would be badly disturbed by it, and for good reason.

In its realism, *Olympia* stood out against the host of fluffy nudes exhibited in the same halls. She was made of flesh and blood, and was so alive that it was unsettling.

Manet came out of the adventure muddied but famous.

In the face of such a wall of hostility, Manet sought comfort from Baudelaire, asking him his opinion.

From his Brussels retreat the poet responded with annoyance, "Do you think you are the first man ever to find himself in this position? Are you more of a genius than Châteaubriand or Wagner? Nonetheless, they too have been the objects of much mockery!"

He added, "You are but the first in the decrepitude of your art".

From afar and on high, away from the buzzing tongues of Paris at once so cruel and so frivolous, Baudelaire was correct in his analysis, identifying the problem which was Manet's alone, but equally of his times which held him hostage.

"The decrepitude of art" was the response given to those who were in power and set the standards of "good taste", clinging to the illusion of beauty even if beauty is not a conceptual matter but rather has to do with moments, chance, coincidence, accidents.

It had become frozen in formulas, petrified. The generation that was to recognize Manet as its master discovered beauty in the painting medium itself; to the same degree that it was tuned into truth and the instant, it would soon be tuned into itself.

It is a great irony that Baudelaire, whose love for Manet had grown out of a misunderstanding and whose anxieties and enthusiasms, repudiations and espousals had been so poorly coordinated, should have cast in a single phrase the seeds of an awesome modernity that he had vested with fascination and allure, while then, in the evening of his life, in his physical and mental decline, he had so lucidly perceived another decline. That of the academic style, the rules and the canons. But at the same time, he transformed the painter into a prophet and a martyr. As bourgeois as he was and (unlike some of his friends) not in the least troubled by material concerns such as the absolute necessity of selling his work to live, Manet was, in his own way, a martyr of art. He wanted to be recognized for what he was. He was not, and he passed from the level of the misunderstood to that of the cursed – the stuff that legendary figures are made of.

A PAINTER OF HISTORY

June 19, 1867. The Austrian emperor's brother Maximilian, crowned emperor of Mexico at the instigation of Napoleon III (who had seen benefits in it for himself), was executed by a firing squad following a wave of nationalist feeling that demanded Mexico for the Mexicans. Thus this part of the American continent was cut loose from the European orbit in which it had lived since the Spanish invasion.

Manet had never been attracted to the painting of history and had always been rather reserved about current events apart from a few sketches of the Paris Commune. Hence, it is curious that this tragic news item constituted in him the source of inspiration for a vast composition that he carried out in several versions. In these his aim was not to arrive at a synthesis of the various experiments, but simply to vary the position of the figures, the overall tone, details of dress, as well as the painting's structural rhythm.

For one of these, through the kind offices of Commandant Lesjone (another habitué of fashionable literary salons), he had a group of soldiers from the Pépinière barracks pose in his studio.

At first Manet had planned to present his first version at the private exhibition he was organizing for the 1867 Exposition Universelle. He was forced to renounce this project because the subject had become taboo, due to the cautious reserve maintained by public opinion in the face of an event that had heaped discredit on Napoleon III and unmasked his international politics.

The version presently held by the museum of Mannheim is doubtlessly the most interesting: its subject matter is strange and is more explicit here than in the others. A compact group of armed soldiers is shown, taking aim and firing at the three men condemned to death (Maximilian and his two generals, Mejia and Miramor, who had unwittingly followed their emperor to their deaths). In contrast to the sharp image of the soldiers, whose uniforms are given importance by the white stripes of the baldrics and the gaiters, the three victims are loosely

grouped and can barely be made out, though the shadows they cast on the ground are, on the other hand, emphatic, suggesting an implacable sun.

A wall cuts diagonally across the scene of the massacre, dividing it from a natural setting whose richness is attested to by the clump of trees (a European species). A crowd of figures crouching near the wall, piled up against one another, forming a loose tangle of arms and gazes, injects the overall composition with a strange quality, as if Manet had mistaken this execution with a sombre corrida. The action could change, but the appearance of the spectators would remain the same.

Critics of his time did not breathe a word about it. When it was finally recognized, on the occasion of its exhibition in America in a Barnum-like circus parade display, the critics perceived only the anecdotal aspect of it, praising its "real interest, as much because of the historical romance of the subject as its inherent eccentricity". This analysis perhaps too readily dismisses the most striking thing in Manet's work, which is the role of voyeur assigned to the spectator, clearly stated in the painting itself.

Manet was a voyeur of history, in spite of himself. He was also its witness at the time of the Commune. A few sketches of the Versailles reprisals have come down to us, which he painted straight from life, on the trail of the rebels.

In them, we can find an echo of the ambiguous theatricality of *The Execution of Maximilian.*

The Exposition Universelle in Paris.
Oslo, Nasjonal galleriet.

THE EXPOSITION UNIVERSELLE OF 1867

The series of Expositions Universelles that punctuated the social and cultural life of the 19th century served to strengthen academicism in the field of the arts, in keeping with the aspirations of the privileged classes of the Second Empire and the Third Republic.

Flaubert had defined them with characteristic brevity in his compendium of foolish quotations, the *Dictionnaire des Idées Reçues*, as the "fad of our times": "Exposition = the collective madness of the 19th century". Since France had entered the era of modernity in a blaze of glory and self-importance, it had to at all times prove itself in the eyes of all and maintain its momentum, at the same time meeting the challenges of very fierce competition. The Exposition Universelle meant above all rivalry. Each nation's honor was at stake as it demonstrated its scientific, technological and artistic assets.

Curiously, the Expositions Universelles brought uniformity to scientific discovery, as well as to current tastes and related production. It is significant that the arena selected for this international confrontation was the Champ de Mars. It was a place packed with symbolic meaning, as well as one that was sufficiently large to hold the many temporary buildings required by such an event. It was the place where a given sector of the French population had become aware of its unity. The mass for the Republican brotherhood had been celebrated there. The Second Empire did not object to wading in the same mud as the sans-culottes.

This muddy parade ground had been transformed into a place of popular assembly, of brotherhood and of confrontation for the cult of ingenuity. From the enlightened 18th century that had overthrown the old and gasping monarchy, wormeaten by its class prejudices, the 19th century inherited a love for science as the expression of democracy inasmuch as it was at the service of man and his future, and it was accessible to all according to a system of values that was no longer based on class but on merit.

Le Déjeuner sur l'Herbe.
Paris, Louvre.

The Expositions Universelles were never anything more than a public demonstration of power. Those of 1855 and 1867 were dedicated to the glory of the Empire, which had reached its peak of fame and power in time for the second of the two.

The Exposition of 1867 reinforced a Paris drunk with its own glory, but at the same time deeply divided. Never had the contrasts been so strongly marked in the city. Haussmann's urbanistic butchery had undermined many of the city's popular rallying points, breeding grounds for resentment, rumbling discontent and hence for revolt. The rabble was driven away from the center, where it had had its dens, escape routes, safe houses and underground networks. It settled in the outskirts of the city. The aristocratic suburb of Saint-Germain, and the ostentatious nouveau riche districts on the Monceau plain contrasted sharply with the shantytown of Vaugirard, the hovels of Grenelle and the slumbelt of Belleville.

The Exposition Universelle was opened for the wealthy classes of Paris, for the right-minded and propertied bourgeoisie, the ones who laid down the law because it was the law of the strongest, so that they could flaunt their consumerism.

Art was just one aspect, so trivial that it was of no use in daily life, of the pragmatic laws in force.

Furthermore, the artists who were the vehicles of new ideas were not welcome. They were troublemakers and potential rebels.

The Expositions Universelles were similar to the Salons, which in fact later occupied the spaces that had been abandoned by the former (such as the Salon de l'Industrie and the Grand Palais, from 1900 on), and upheld the aesthetics of such artists as Cabanel, Bouguereau, Gérôme, Bonnat, Carolus-Duran, Dagnan Bouveret, and well above the fray, his imperial majesty, the great Meissonier, the most expensive painter of his time.

The idea of dynamic progress, of technological and scientific discovery was applied in equal measure to the plastic arts. It was not a new idea, but it had been distorted, since it was based entirely on the idea of an acquired skill. Hence all individuality was repressed in the name of the canons of art professed by the School, which was increasingly tyrannical in its hold over minds and institutions.

It was the School which determined all stages in an artist's life: the learning process (Ecole des Beaux-Arts, Prix de Rome), the opportunity to exhibit (the Salon), and to be recognized (distribution of awards). It even set the fashions, since it was the Académie which provided the links between artists, society and private patrons.

The Exposition Universelle of 1855 celebrated Ingres and Delacroix, uniting in glory the two opposite trends in art. But it rejected Courbet (who is now recognized as having made history), because his realism shocked the morally good. He was thus reduced to presenting his works in a booth in the immediate neighborhood of the official exhibition. This was seen as an act of provocation.

At the 1867 Exposition Universelle, he repeated this move, followed this time by Manet, in an assertion of his independence.

Refusing the offers of a jury that included Cabanel, Pils, Gérôme, Bida, Fromentin, Baudry, Théodore Rousseau, Jules Breton and Meissonier, Manet decided to organize his own exhibition, his "personal Louvre", as Courbet had called it.

At his own expense, he had a booth constructed on a piece of land belonging to the Marquis de Pomereux, on the corner of Montaigne and Alma Avenues, which at the time was up for sale and was quite free of other buildings.

He charged fifty centimes for the privilege of seeing the fifty paintings, three museum copies and three etchings presented together with a catalogue whose introduction explained this arrogant stance:

"Since 1861, Monsieur Manet has exhibited or tried to exhibit. This year he has decided to show his works directly to the public. His first exhibitions at the Salon were well met by the public but in later years he was so frequently rejected that he began to

Portrait of Zola. (detail).
Paris, Louvre.

Portrait of Zola.
Paris, Louvre.

think that if one's endeavors in art are a battle, at least they should be fought with equal arms. This means exhibiting what one has done".

The public was invited to see "sincere works". "It is the quality of sincerity that gives these works a tone of protest, even though the painter's sole objective was to render his impressions".

It would appear that at the time no one took notice of this frank and obvious reference to the impression as something sufficient unto itself and capable of justifying a work of art.

Instead it was a matter of great importance to the artist, and was what stood between him and public recognition.

It was illustrated by the canvases that he exhibited: *The Absinthe Drinker, Déjeuner sur l'Herbe, Young Man in Majo Costume, Victorine Meurent in Espada Costume, The Tragic Actor*, and *The Fifer* (all works that had been refused by the Salon); then, *The Spanish Singer, Dead Christ with Angels, Olympia, Christ Insulted by the Soldiers* (works which had been through the Caudine Forks of the jury); and, finally, *Musiques aux Tuileries, The Reading, Boy with Sword, The Spanish Ballet, The Old Musician, The Street Chanteuse, Lola de Valence, Reclining Young Woman in Spanish Dress* and *Departure from the Port du Boulogne* (paintings which had already been shown at a solo exhibition at the Martinet gallery).

According to Antonin Proust, it was dazzling, but he was a longstanding and loyal friend. The public was less indulgent and less admiring, to the point of undisguised laughter: "All those whom Paris counts among its self-proclaimed top artists rallied to meeting at the Manet exhibition. It was a concert of raving pot-bellied men. The press was unanimous or almost unanimous in seconding them. Never at any time has there been such a revolting show of injustice".

In the midst of this uproar, only one note of approval was to be heard, deep and penetrating. It was that of Zola, who had written a series of newspaper articles surveying art of the 19th century. They were published in a volume that was widely read.

It was illustrated with a portrait of the artist by Braquemond and an etching done after the Olympia. It cost two francs and "sold like hotcakes".

When his column in *L'Evènement* was discontinued, Zola took up the defense of his friend.

His enthusiasm and commitment had gotten him dismissed from his post, as the paper had risked losing its subscribers if it continued to publish his "wild imaginings."

It was considered a wild imagining to say: "I endeavored to place Monsieur Manet in the position he deserves, at the top. People may have laughed at the panegyrist as much as they did at the painter. One day both of us will have our vindication. It is not possible – not possible, I say – that Monsieur Manet will not have his day of triumph, when he will outshine all the insignificant mediocrity that surrounds him".

For a young writer, a starting journalist, this statement did not lack in gallantry, with its invective, its conviction, so boldly flourished that it must have annoyed before it convinced.

Zola also openly criticized the common enemy, the jury responsible for rejecting such a great artist. "I bluntly accuse the jury in force this year of bias. I have no problems in declaring that I admire Monsieur Manet, and I confess that I set little store by all Monsieur Cabanel's face powder and by far prefer the pungent and holy perfumes of true nature". Already in this assured and nude affirmation, we can sense the flame of satire kindling in Zola, which would reach its full development in *J'Accuse*. Some parallels can be drawn between Manet in disgrace and Dreyfus, who had been repudiated by the same society. "I defended Manet as I will defend all my life any example of open individuality that comes under attack. I will always be on the side of the vanquished".

By attacking the intolerance of a jury, Zola was attacking the crimes of a class whose turpitude,

vices and narrow-mindedness he was awakening to, and would describe in his works.

In the name of aesthetics and friendship, Zola had already mounted the horse of dissent. He was to tilt against the public authorities and regimes which by relying on the support of the hated bourgeoisie strengthened the latter's hold over minds and bodies.

Manet was just the opening stake in a political crusade.

THE TEMPTATIONS OF ART ARE A BATTLE

In a rather formal statement, colored with weariness, but also resolute in its painful lucidity, Manet raised a novel question. It was necessary to struggle if one wanted to gain recognition. "The temptations of art are a battle", he wrote at the opening of the catalogue he drew up for his 1867 exhibition.

Such an idea was totally new at the time, and no doubt Manet's generation was the first to have to confront this problem and at the same time to manage its recently acquired independence from the institutions.

Until then, the artist had almost always been in the service of a patron power. A paid employee, he served the cause of his patron and his art was above all a tool for propaganda. His subjects were dictated by the demands of his job. He was required less "to be" than to serve. And if his art survived the centuries it was thanks more to the weight of his personality than to the constraints to which his post had made him subject. The subject mattered little then – Madonna with the Christ Child or the Life of the Saints if on the side of the church, and the glory of the king, if on the side of the Court – if the painter managed to overcome the inherent restrictions of his post and to express himself in some way, his passions, his desires, his fantasies. In interpreting such works, the subject is overlooked in order to focus solely on the "technique" and the revealing details.

Manet's problem (which was behind the loathing he aroused) was that he interpreted subjects that no political system could vindicate. Not only did he want to break away from the canons of the School, but also from the standards of representation that were confined to a range of subjects which had become trite. Painting's services were no longer required by the Church and the State, so it turned to the service of cultural ideas born of a society that, ever since the Revolution had hoisted it into power, had harbored an old nostalgia for Antiquity, perhaps in the hope that some of its prestige and glory would rub off on it.

Besides the Greek robe rendered in the academic style, gradually emptied of all meaning, painting was founded on a basic morality that stood somewhere between patriotism (which the fall of the Empire exacerbated) and a return to the origins (which in fact had remained a constant motif running through French mythology).

The realism that was born of this was seen as an affront to the dignity of man. Millet and Courbet dared to paint even nature in the sombre colors of effort, poverty, pain and a hostility that society would not admit. The only vision that it recognized then was that of Jules Breton: a cheap imitation of nature, the kind of reconstruction offered by light opera. Manet's realism was also an insult to the dignity of a society that hid behind the "academies", and preferred to a truly nude woman in a natural setting with an ordinary type of man, a woman whose nudity referred back to that of the goddesses of antiquity and of the "she dressed in her nudity" ready-to-wear-type.

Manet was still painting in the studio because he had not yet cleared the hurdle that would lead him to the *plein air*. This would require a few new acquaintances, passionate arguments and the example of younger painters who, while still recognizing him as their master, would show him the way to his true destiny and real vocation.

Manet was "rescued" by the painters who were to become the Impressionists though at the time he made nothing of their aesthetic. He still took his reference from the museums, and was torn between respect for his culture and an increasingly strong attraction to "modernity".

Much like Degas, Manet's revolution was less formal than it was intellectual. It was the content of his paintings that was essentially revolutionary.

This content was concerned with only his instincts, his personality, his dreams, his obsessions and his fears.

His art relied on no props, while all around him the whole world hid itself behind the trimmings of pictorial conventions passed from generation to generation like a talisman.

His temptations in art were not inspired by the competitive spirit that spurred his detractors. They were not the result of an experience made to project its fruit as a response to received learning but the spontaneous development of his sensibilities in the face of the reality of his time, and plunging to the depth of his soul, giving to his painting the powerful impact of confession.

This projection of a self awakened to reality made way in the world, but it resembled the Way of the Cross, complete with stations and its martyrology. A sublime example of mythological dimensions is van Gogh, who represents pain made into a daily bread. Manet did not paint his pain, but his pleasures, his sensations. He did not hide behind the false decorum of the ateliers, but he offered plain and simple reality, where he found himself at peace, with the intensity of his dreams, contemplation and life-giving energy, before a woman, a piece of fruit or nature. Hence the extraordinary simplicity of his style, the lack of decoration, the harsh austerity that lets his subject stand out and projects it onto our consciousness, while the trappings of the picturesque used by the painters of the day delighted the eye as it filtered out the intelligence, the conscience of the painting.

Manet's works go straight to their mark.

They have no object or person to defend them, nor any charming details, nor any reassuring or prestigious references.

Before the court of public opinion, Manet treated his art with such total commitment that his contemporaries found it disturbing. And they convicted him for it.

Lilac Bouquet.
Berlin, Staatliche Museen.

Portrait of Madame Jacob.
Paris, Louvre.

Horse Races at Longchamps.
Chicago, Art Institute.

Manet's studio, 4 Rue St. Pétersbourg.

THE BALCONY

It was Fantin-Latour who introduced Berthe Morisot to Manet. She was at the Louvre, copying a Rubens. She was taken by the painter's charm, and his aura of a somewhat stormy and cursed celebrity. On his part, Manet was dazzled by the grace of the young woman, who was then 27 years old possessed of the natural poise of the noble born paired with the reserve of the well-bred.

Of all the women whose company Manet enjoyed, Berthe Morisot – she was to be the wife of Manet's brother – was the one on whose friendship he could rely, thanks in part to their shared interests in art and preference for the *plein air* (to which no doubt Berthe Morisot had initiated him). She had arrived at just the right moment in Manet's life, as he had been planning to do a composition on the theme of the balcony and invited her to pose as one of the figures; the others were Fanny Claus, a young musician who was thrilled with the idea of posing, Antoine Guillemet, a painter with whom Berthe Morsot had worked closely at Auvers-sur-l'Oise, and lastly Léon Koella who played a minor role in the painting, his silhouette merging into the shadows of the room with the other three figures inscribed in a rather ostentatious hieratic line-up framed by the balcony and its decoration of flowers in the lefthand angle.

Manet painted the figures individually and then did a first version to prepare the placement of the figures (Fanny Claus is the closest to the balustrade, seated).

The Balcony became one of Manet's most famous paintings, and justifiably so, but it is also one of his most enigmatic.

Using an unusually rigorous composition, Manet made the group compact while at the same time highlighting the figure of Morisot, who radiates her own personality. A long cascade of frothy white fabric offsets the structure and rhythm of the green of the balustrade and the energetic line of the fan held by the seated woman.

Guillemet and Claus form a pair in counterpoint playing on the striking, almost geometric contrast

of black and white. The female figure is of a sculpturesque whiteness, while the male figure recedes into the background shadows, into which the figure of Koella has completely disappeared. It is a prodigious use of lighting effects that establishes the hierarchy of the figures, highlighting Berthe Morisot. She was just one of the many female figures whose beauty Manet enhanced, rendering homage to the fragile tenderness of their flesh and their radiance, the intensity of their gaze, the exquisite grace of a natural pose, the radiance of a complete sensuality that never even hints at the mysogynist heaviness of Degas' lewd nudes or the complacent bestiality of Renoir's. Manet gives them a dimension of civility which could be the expression of his cultural level, the class which produced him, but most of all it is a different way of perceiving women. This is an epoch that proclaimed its favor of women, but only *en dishabillé* for purposes of questionable taste, indeed shamelessly exploiting the female figure for more or less confessable ends.

Manet's adulation took the form of reserve, a distance taken out of respect for the model, but at the same time celebrating her, exalting her, and giving her the opportunity to be herself, making of her a partner, and no longer an object to be shaped at will. Contrary to Degas, who saw his models with a heavy and cruel gaze, and painted them in risqué poses with the realism of a voyeur, Manet was too respectful of the "other" to dissect her with such ruthless cruelty.

Though it was prepared in the studio of Rue Guyot, the balcony of Rue Saint Pétersbourg was where the final version of the painting was carried out. The pointed ostentation of the figures' bearing, their clothing, the overall expression of grandeur and a sort of superiority transformed the balcony scene into a sort of parade of worldly values. It could have just as well been the dress circle of the Opéra, where the spectators themselves become part of the spectacle.

Georges Bataille said that Manet was "one of the most reticent painters, who can be penetrated only with difficulty. He was the most worthy herald of the birth of the magical world, so rich in surprises, that modern painting today reveals to our gaze". Indeed, an artist such as Magritte was deeply troubled by this painting, sensitive as he was to the question of "semblance" and the fundamental ambiguity between reality and how to show it.

Furthermore, the balcony, by architectural definition and function, is a place for seeing, where while remaining in the comfort one's own home, it is possible to see the outside, to contemplate it, to witness the unexpected.

Manet's *Balcony* also creates a space in which the figures are in full regalia, dressed to be seen. They become actors, though they are defined as spectators. Manet undermined this definition by endowing the figures with such a strong presence that they seem inquisitors. The great curiosity they show, which leaves no point on the horizon unguarded is disturbing. Berthe Morisot looks toward the left and Guillemet towards the right, while Fanny Claus confronts us with self-assured impertinence. Nevertheless, on account of their strong presence, the figures occupy the space of the painting and assert themselves for what they are, becoming the focus of interest – bringing us full circle round to the starting definition of the painting as a spectacle.

Thus, by a trick of reciprocity that makes the painting's characters alternate their roles within the painting, they become actors. But if we take full note of what we are looking at, we become aware that these characters are observing a spectacle, one which entirely eludes us, about which we will never know anything. Finally, though a spectacle presupposes a stationary or expectant pose, at least two of the actors in the *Balcony* are in a stance of departure. Gloved, hatted and even prudently armed with an umbrella, Fanny Claus may well not have appeared on the balcony until the moment in which she had decided to leave the room hidden to us by

the darkness. And the man towering over her with that tall and proud bearing that we ascribe to the close of luncheons, accompanies her.

In fact, the departure here recalls another departure, that depicted in the admirable *Déjeuner*. This painting was so carefully executed that it can be compared to a 17th-century Dutch painting, rich in domestic details, the lustrous faience ware, the elegant transparence of the crystal and the mellow glon of the yellow lemons set against the whiteness of the starched tableloth.

That vision of opulence has been interrupted by something that eludes us. One man is seated at the table, hat on his head. He is still drinking. We imagine that he is lingering before his departure, while the maid is shown halted in her tracks, carafe in hand as though captured by a photographer's flash, or perhaps arrested at the sight of something which is hidden to our view, as in the other painting. As in the *Balcony*, a decorative element counterbalances the rigor of the composition. In the *Balcony* it is a plant with decorated planter; in the *Déjeuner*, it is a coat of arms and, following Chardin's example, a large bowl with a geometric design at once mysterious and soft. The central figure is a man in a dark jacket and light-colored trousers, wearing a tightly knotted tie, his head covered with a straw hat. He leans on the table, suggesting his departure. He is relaxed (or reserved) and weary, yet at the same time the tilt of his head and faraway gaze show determination.

The Lion Hunter.
Saõ Paolo, Museum of Art.

Photograph of Manet.

Under the contemptuous pickaxe of the Baron Haussmann, a given Paris disappeared and another was born.

All that made it picturesque disappeared. All that was considered its grandeur appeared.

The style of the period leaned towards ostentation rather than the picturesque. The planner attacked the city as if it were a virgin forest, a very old forest, very venerable, with many species of trees and permeated with odors, crisscrossed with roads thick with mud and poverty, where crime and love walked hand in hand. It was a Paris in which traditions were so old and anchored in time that the meaning of their origins had been lost. Time flowed with a continuity that all Haussmann's renovations cut short.

It was a black and dour Paris, but rich in mystique. A city that someone like Gérard de Nerval loved to explore, as though it were a labyrinth in which he would find Death, like a destiny. A Paris of alleyways which provided a continuous supply of victims to the gallows. Between the sidewalk and the gallows there was a gap measured by a class who could not find peace with society. The society of the day dreamed of nothing but grandeur, traced along the lines that it itself had imposed. It saw in this Medieval Paris a city of the Dark Ages. It felt the threat of the commoners' longstanding resentment at every turn and was frightened.

Haussmann's urban plan was also a police action, a political program.

He was lauded by the people of the handsome quarters which he had erected in the architectural exuberance of his time, where opulence was also perceived as comfort. This built-up side of Paris, the west, abandoned the east side to those who did not share in the extraordinary economic development that had made the former possible. Haussmann's work was to provide the backdrop to the life of ceremony and ritual that took form under the Second Empire and was perpetuated by the Third Republic. Only World War I would succeed in bringing to an end the worldly luxuriance that became legendary as the "Belle Epoque".

When Manet did not draw inspiration for his paintings from museum pieces, he turned to the imagery of this Paris, rustling and deliciously tawdry.

It was a Paris born of real estate speculation and the growth of colonialism, a Paris that fashioned itself the image of the modern city.

Until this time, Paris had been a conglomerate, rather clumsy and random, of villages that had absorbed one another by their growth, but which retained their autonomy and even their character. Here and there bits of city could be glimpsed, like stage sets, uprights in a theatre where one could look into the wings. Moreover, the great civic projects were approached in terms of appearances. The façade to the Place des Vosges and to the Place Vendôme were erected and behind the unity of the stageset, the houses were waiting to be built.

In the name of pomp, the Place Saint-Sulpice had to meet the same fate, under Servandoni.

Napoleon III did not always manage to avoid this precedent (Rue de Rivoli), but the concept of urbanism that he upheld was focused on the handling of the masses, a block of houses, an entire district. It was a more ambitious vision than his predecessors', and more restricting for the occupant. A framework for his life was imposed on him. Show was nice, but what it hid was also important.

There was nothing to hide. Never had houses been designed with such attention to detail. Even the opulence displayed on the façade – the ornaments, sculptures, friezes, cornices and caryatids – had their continuation on the interior.

Buildings were constructed for handsomeness and comfort. Opulence was no longer mere appearance. It was a daily experience.

Art contributed to its splendor and development. Many painters and sculptors worked "on commission," adapting to the architectural requirements. They were wonderful and prolific craftsmen

of comfort, as well as the hawkers of the period's dreams. This assured them both of their reputation in society and abundant commissions, which favored the rapid development and diffusion of a style.

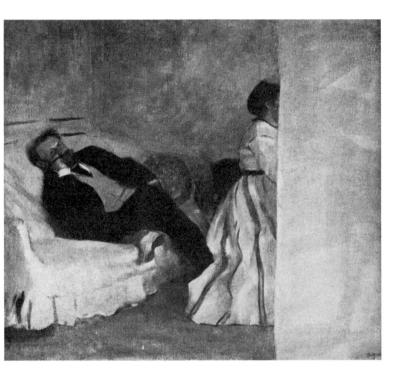

It may be considered a miraculous coincidence that at the very moment in which Paris was engaged in the most far-reaching renovation project it had ever known, photography had just been invented and was able to record this awesome metamorphosis, offering to posterity a "before" and "after", that are the two gauges of a political orientation and a birth, that of modern Paris.

Under the driving force of a regime that intended to socialize with the rigor of a dictatorship and to create the double utopia of a city suited to promoting the well-being of all and a home for everyone, Paris became a city that conformed to the standards of modernity.

On one side, some enthusiastic hikers, Marville, Charles Négre and Baldus by name, wandered through the city with their fantastic gear, framing shots of the Medieval streets that were to be transformed into squares, boulevards, looming administrative complexes, military barracks. Paradoxically, photography, which is a product of technological progress, hastened to record what was destined to disappear, orienting itself towards a past which would enter the present as ruins and demolition sites.

The ruins were just an incidental part of the condemned past, shown, however with tenderness and lucidity.

Painters who were contemporaries of these photographers and this phenomenon painted the vitality and charm of the city living in the present, almost never revealing the shades of the past.

Unlike the famous landscape artists of the 18th century, who applied themselves to the depiction of ruin sites with an alarmed concern before the lessons that they drew from these visions, the painters of the city that was making itself, and making ruins of itself, turned their backs on these ruins in favor of a genuine inquiry into the soul of the promised city, already the setting for a life that they rejoiced in.

The Impressionists extracted from this turbulent,

Femme à la Jarretière.
Copenhagen, Museum of Ordrupgaarde.

Portrait of Victorine Meurent.
Private collection.

ardent, frivolous Paris (pleased with its power and glamour) visions that aimed at objectivity. They were witnesses, without for all that denying, repudiating, or abandoning what gave them their individuality, their style, their handwriting, through which their painting became a trial ground for the experience itself of painting.

They interpreted what they saw. But they also tried to interpret the movement of the city as the expression of its daily reality (and this was to culminate in Futurism).

The city finds expression as a city as much in its people as in its monuments. One does not exist without the other. One of them taken alone (the city emptied of its inhabitants) results in a vision that is outside of reality, a fiction. This found its highest expression in de Chirico's metaphysical painting. The gaze that Manet and his friends and contemporaries turned on their city as it was taking shape was neither self-indulgent nor gratuitous. It was not objective, but rather in perfect harmony with the instant. The instant was as much the subject of the canvas as it was its backdrop. Manet avoided painting the crowds that he loved to lose himself in, with the hustle-bustle – charming, futile and at times vulgar, though also distinguished in many respects – of the Boulevard, the period's greatest "salon". People rubbed shoulders there, lingering over witty conversation, coquetry, trysts and intrigues. Manet loved its loose morals and studied elegance, the sign of civility. And of civilization. But he did not draw inspiration from it for his subjects nor his technique. He left the long zoom shots from atop balconies overlooking the colorful crowds to Monet and Pissarro, which they used to inject their canvases with charming energy. He was not interested in reportage.

Manet was a participant, not a witness, in Parisian life. He no longer sought to eternalize its "characters", (the laundresses and ironers) as Degas did with crude naturalism.

Strangely, Manet, who had never been on the side of the dream merchants creating illusions from their studios, also turned away from those who could just as well have utilized photography to capture what they saw.

Manet too reconstructed the world in his studio. He remained at length within its walls, only embracing the *plein air* technique very late in his career, when he had already made his most important contributions to art working in the studio with his carefully arranged scenes, using a conception of reality that had become distorted in a way that he relentlessly sought to reverse, pouring his energy into countering its excessess, its absurdity and its self-indulgence with the harshness of a reality recomposed.

L'Olympia, Le Déjeuner sur l'Herbe, and *The Balcony* are scenes that have been staged as if in a photography studio. In this sense, Manet's technique could be considered interchangeable with that of photography.

And yet, Manet did not show an excessive interest in this art. Without knowing much about it, he had borrowed some of its techniques, and some of its strengths, such as that of giving order to the world, and going beyond the aim of objectivity by steeping it in the strangeness that lies just below the surface of the most banal, conventional subjects.

THE MODEL IN THE GREENHOUSE

Manet was only an occasional *plein air* painter, since he was more attracted to the model whom he could pose at will in his studio.

Victorine was his most frequent visitor in Rue Goyot during his years of struggle. But he never painted her as she was, only as he envisioned her. At times as a perversely lascivious odalisque, at times in Spanish costume, and once even as the determined and yet sardonic Fifer, when the model he had initially selected, a young soldier, did not meet his needs.

Modeling is an art, an emotional and intellectual complicity with the painter, a sort of dialogue, whereas portraiture merely requires its subject to be himself, and above all to not pose. Manet confirmed this by telling his portrait subjects, "Move around, smile, wander, let yourself go. The more you move around, the better it is".

Berthe Morisot was the first in a series of portraits of exquisite femininity. In them, Manet let the tender admiration he felt for her, and later for Mery Laurent and Eva Gonzales, show. He was soon painting her in everyday poses; for her, this meant in the act of painting, which she did under his guidance. This fantastic succession of women in bloom in his studio turned Manet into a sort of worldly portraitist – worldly because at least in this field he gained recognition, and especially because he was painting the people of his own world, the artsy, liberal bourgeoisie which rubbed elbows with a certain part of the aristocracy which was anxious to shake off the centuries of stagnation that weighed on it, along with the complexes born of the Revolution.

Confronted with a shining, ambitious bourgeoisie, the aristocracy's only option was to compete with that class on its own turf: seduction, with women as the focal point of social and high society life. Marcel Proust had only to unleash a Madame Verdurin to put the bourgeoisie in its place, or the Countess Greffulhe, who bore only a modest title but was a managing woman, keenly aware of her social role. The beauty attributed to her was one of her weapons, and her good taste another. Wit was not overlooked and could bridge the gap of financial standing, since it was considered elegant to surround oneself with intellectuals.

Social life at the end of the 19th century came strangely close to resembling that of the 18th century, where the women were the driving force and wit was the coin in use.

For Manet, the problem was not posed in terms of revolution, but as the acknowledgment of the facts. He was tied to this society which upheld academicism, money and learning; his class had condemned him to be of that school of thinking. That he came through it unscathed was as much a miracle as it was thanks to his personality which was clear of cultural prejudice. People advised him to go after official awards, and he did not object. Indeed, he aspired to this bombastic form of recognition.

The fact of having been rejected repeatedly, an intruder, increased his stature in the eyes of those who made him their master (more in a moral sense than pictorial), an unwitting symbol of their struggle against the institutions, they urged him to "take the leap" across the void between him and total, absolute modernity in painting. An irreversible step, but one which he too sensed was the inevitable destiny of painting, though he saw it from the perspective of the Louvre, and not that of the Seine or the suburb of Argenteuil. The problem came to a head when, painting subjects of his own class, and even set in the most conventional, fashionable environments so prized by Baudelaire (who was soon to fade from the scene, and in any case was no longer able to offer the support that the painter so much needed), Manet put his finger on something outside of the usual setting that his subjects stepped into and there remained. The polite neutrality of the settings exploded into a thrill of modernity, made up repressed sensuality, controlled and lucid refinement, and at times a twinge of nostalgia, as though his paintbrush in depicting beauty and happiness already had an awareness of the fragility of its subject.

Manet would change studios many times, but never his way of honoring his beautiful guests.

He left Rue Guyot and in 1872 moved to a room in 4 Rue Saint-Pétersbourg (today Rue Léningrad) whose four windows offered a generous view of Rue de Berne and the westside railway tracks.

He then chose a room not far from there, at 77 Rue d'Amsterdam, but before it was ready he had to settle for the studio, number 70 of the same street, of an acquaintance, the Swedish painter Rosen. It was there that he painted *Monsieur and Madame Guillemet in the Greenhouse.*

It is a rigorously constructed work, plainly laid out, depicting a couple of his friends. No doubt, Manet respected the canons of the genre which called for an effective physical resemblance to those who posed with the idea of immortalizing themselves on canvas in mind. All the more so, since the couple were close friends of the painter. Both of them were very much in the eye of fashion, among the most talked-about representatives of the period's high society.

But, with their agreement, Manet also let the setting play its role. Rosen's studio also included a winter garden with a very special atmosphere. A painter's studio in this period was a true work of art in itself, as much a showroom and personal museum as a workplace. It was a space suited to the many receptions that painters were obliged to organize, as the art dealer network was in its infant stage, and was not enough alone to ensure the sale of paintings. Manet amused himself by refining the theatrical character of the place and the decorative effect of the plants. The bench that Madame Guillemet is seated upon with her husband leaning over it is a rhythmic device, much like the balustrade in *The Balcony* and the railing in *The Railroad.* It offers an almost geometrical rhythm in a space enlivened by the movement of the plants. Much as in *Chez le Père Lathuille,* the attentive posture of the man is emphasized, with broad brushstrokes in the latter, whereas in *Madame and Monsieur Guillemet* Manet

focused on the elegant, worldly character of his subjects. They are depicted wearing clothes and in a pose that was designed to flatter a public opinion that was highly sensitive to a work's contents. In fact, the critics did not fail to notice this when it was presented at the 1879 Salon. They declared with the satisfaction of those whose advice has been heeded that Manet was no longer the "bloodthirsty revolutionary". Early on, Manet had been branded with the image of a man given over to violence, and the public had confused him with the socialist Courbet, a destroyer of the bourgeoisie and active participant in the defeat of the Vendôme corps. Courbet had just died, and Manet rendered him posthumous homage in a vibrant and realistic portrait.

Had Manet been subdued? It is easy to picture him slipping into the skin of one of those official artists who at the time waited patiently to work on one of those grand renovation sites that the Third Republic had opened all over Paris, welcoming the age of prosperity and expunging the sackage of the Commune. The Hôtel de Ville in Paris was one of the most notable of these projects. Its decor required the work of a great many artists. Manet failed to be included among them, though he would have liked to have been. A letter bears witness to this, but he received no answer.

Had he been given the chance, there is no doubt that he would have produced a pictorial poem of a vision that was perfectly in tune with the rhythms of modernity and the daily life to which he was perfectly suited to act as the bard.

A painter must be in step with his own times and paint what he sees. Though it is straightforward, Manet's proposal was not easily understood by minds inclined to mystification, and 19th-century painting was victim of its patrons who had charged it with a social mission.

Painting was the vehicle for messages to the public, in which the painters used to excess a sequence of codes and conventions that were accessible to the latter. This may seem at odds with the idea of respecting the canons of art. It is possible to see in the 19th century a sort of inflation of the content of the subjects whose primary significance deepened progressively. They were extreme, excessive, in sentiment. Never had painting been so sentimental as in the close of this century, where the masses, having failed to achieve wealth, were moved to tears by the finer feelings that art fostered with skillful generosity.

In the 18th century this sentimentality was the exclusive ground of an aristocracy that had grown weak at its foundations and was vaguely aware of its inevitable demise. In the hands of the ruling bourgeoisie, it took on a quasi-religious meaning. It was a substitute for vacillating faith, which had been undermined by the rampant Positivism of the period.

For those who were receptive to it, who indulged themselves in it, it was a sort of solemn invocation of their willing poverty, where the wounds were soothed by the spreading perception of poverty as a fateful coincidence, a promoter of virtue and a common ground, where the merciful rich turned their attention to the poor. The generally accepted idea that there are class differences, but that this injustice can be overcome with solidarity was of comfort.

Painting, a tool of bourgeois politics, fueled this notion, upholding it with a sickeningly indulgent iconography. Reality was outrageously falsified in the name of principles drummed into the people's heads, starting with their schooling. Even patriotism was manipulated as the ferment of a willing sacrifice. Social unity was exalted, the cementing agent of a collectivity that did not share its assets, but only its duties. And the prestige of a flag.

The only escape for those who were condemned from birth to this no-exit situation was the dream.

It was an era of great dreamers, and great escapes toward the unknown. The road was already charted out for the likes of Lautréamont, Rimbaud, Gauguin.

In the same way, the time was ripe for a metamorphosis of pictorial imagery that was nourished on dreams (Redon, Moreau), when people tired of imagery based on an illusion of a reality founded in dubious principles, and nothing else. Ordinary life offered quite a contrasting picture.

This new pictorial imagery was rejected by those in power: they feared it, the wealthy were perhaps put to shame by it, and the victims themselves of society rejected it, showing a remarkable humility in the face of their fate.

Nevertheless, there were some who called for a coming to awareness of this situation. They wished to point out its most ordinary aspects. The most lucid thinkers of the time sought to denounce both the injustice of the system and the people's passive acceptance of it, taking as their model everyday experience. Not that they preached insurrection, but simply consciousness, an arm of the weak.

As bizarre as this seems, Millet and Courbet's testimony was perceived as scandalous in an environment where indulgence had permeated everywhere and the official painters reveled in it. Scorned and condemned to a life of semi-clandestinity, they embraced the cause of a class that had no contact with real painting but only with a form of mystified imagery, the vulgarized version of official painting: chromolithographs.

In the Middle Ages, in the name of religious faith the people were given the right to direct access to the art of their time: it was exhibited in religious buildings that were open to all. Now, in the 19th century, the people no longer had access to anything but an art codified by the ruling powers who manipulated

information and falsified ideology to keep them in a state of ignorance. This allowed them to perpetuate the conventions that they had established through a mythology that they had created for their own ends, eliminating any possibility to break the moral code that passed for law.

Any direction in art that evaded these structures was considered dangerous. Any attempt at usurpation, infiltration or distortion of the imagery in use was severely censured by the law and it was boycotted.

Manet's solitary road could only have been perceived as threatening in such a context.

Paradoxically, even though he clung to museum models (not because of social discipline or opportunism, but rather because he saw in them the logic of an evolution that would have been left incomplete if he broke with the past), Manet was soon seen as dangerous. And because of this, he soon became grist for the critics' mill (those critics who could not admit that art was getting out of their control). Having exhausted the themes offered by the museums, when he moved on to tackle the problem of expressing reality, the affront to public decency was not far in the offing. By stripping reality of its veil of modesty and substituting the figures of a worn mythology with those of everyday reality, Manet was only retreating from a manufactured form of ideology to a gaze whose objectivity under normal circumstances should have passed for innocuous. His painting bore no messages, unlike that of Courbet, who flirted with socialism, or Millet, who tended to interpret the Gospel as a sweet democracy's Tables of the Law. There was nothing of the sort in Manet's work, as he was more concerned with optical problems than with ideological content, and he turned to reality out of lack of imagination. He was not driven by a desire to undermine the social structures (when indeed he stood in the camp of the privileged), but rather by an internal logic that ever since the recent invention of photography demanded that painting hold its ground in

Isabelle Lemonnier.
Paris, Louvre.

The Seine at Argenteuil.
London, Courtauld Institute.

the world of the visible, and not be rendered obsolete.

This was not a remarkable expression of public protest about the reality, but rather concerned the immediate, in terms of the subject above all, and secondarily in terms of style.

This twofold vision of reality was to blame for the distance that separated him, on the threshold of Impressionism, from accepted painting, of which he very much wished to be a part, even if only at the pathetic level of official awards. He first approached his interpretation of reality from the standpoint of museum traditions, later passing to a fullscale revolt, which was not in his nature. His vision of reality blossomed into a style – a brushstroke, a palette – which reflected an increasing involvement with the world and its sensual concreteness; it reflected the subtle modulations of a sensitivity in tune with its surroundings, according to an optical perception that involved a transcription of the sensation through effects. These effects were seen as destructive of the image, while the painter aimed to render its complexity, its transience to the point of disintegrating the object. To achieve this image of truth, Manet had to elude the graphic and pictorial stuctures that confined it and emptied it diminishing its value when he aimed at expressing a global effect. He succeeded, taking as his subject the most ordinary, familiar things, of his world and of his time.

Madame Manet at the Piano and *The Reading* are contemporary. Two canvases whose subject is private life, presided over by a calmly majestic woman as she listens to the mysterious things that surround her, and inject her with life. Music and literature are two components of the rhythm of a lifestyle leisurely enough to permit their cultivation. These are two visions of bourgeois life, so familiar to the painter, in which we can also see the joy of living that describes the 19th century.

This is a vision of reality that has been traditional in painting, each century offering in its own way the testimony of its period, the setting, the clothing, even the personality of its subjects. The reality.

That is because it offers a realistic vision of a given period, in conformity with the customs, manners and milieus. The effective contribution of the painter was all the more determinant because of the banality of the subject, and because he had only to look around him to find it. He could not count on the strength of the subject, its uniqueness, its strangeness or novelty to create a work of art; for this he had to make use of his own inventive.

The subject was merely a pretext for the painter's invention. Madame Manet at the piano shares very closely (if not conventionally) in this bourgeois intimism so suited to painting because it offers a precise framework, narrow but doubly rich in plastic resonance.

There is also plastic resonance in the lustre of the furnishings, the quality of the objects and even the bearing of the pianist, composing a peaceful harmony, not lacking in a touch of luxury. The vision is not at all picturesque and is entirely based on its quality of pleasure rendered by a brushstroke enhanced by this tenderness, this interiorization of things that fosters a sensual vision of the real. The painting resonates with the musical notes, the carefully chosen words of a poem, the exquisiteness of a sensation with all of its vibrations, a dimension of memory and sensuality that underlies its effectiveness, an awakening awareness.

The Reading.
Paris, Louvre.

Portrait of Berthe Morisot.
Private collection.

In *Madame Manet at the Piano*, the painter has given rhythm to the canvas through the mass of the objects that structure and occupy the space. In *The Reading* everything is exploded, starting with the objects, which have disappeared.

The woman is seated on a couch covered in the same material that her dress is made of. Around her a halo of light becomes the true subject of the painting. The reader, in a darker corner of the painting, is merely an accessory to the scene. An anecdotal element, plastically speaking, he is a mere counterpoint. The woman, on the other hand, is attentive, in the passive pose of one who listens to a reading, her delicately complected face intent, and her reddish-blond hair lending a point of intensity to the cascading flow of gauzy white curtains that ends in a slight swell at the bottom of the painting, rippling in the breeze, like softly agitated water. The painting shows the atmosphere of an aquarium: air and water.

In painting this intimate scene, Manet was letting himself slide imperceptibly toward the world of the elements.

In these two paintings, where the painter has added nothing to his usual repertoire of subjects, it may be possible to identify the passage from a painting style that was still in the full grips of the museum influence, not exactly classical but solid in tone and technique, towards a pictorial handling whose boldness rivalled that of Impressionism, which was just then taking form, without Manet but following in his wake of adventure.

Between 1872 and 1874 Manet painted a continuous parade of his women-flowers, while Impressionism was just appearing on the artistic scene. It took the form of a coherent and organized club, certainly exposed to the digs of the critics, but rejected as a group rather than individually. The portrait of Berthe Morisot in a black hat illustrates forcefully and clearly a sensuality, a uniqueness and an assurance that others rarely achieved around him, in a free style that describes the quickening of tenderness, the calm beauty of the flesh, femininity as he perceived it.

Mallarmé was soon to catch up with him. Without denying or betraying the effective presence of the beings and the things that entered into his field of vision, Manet favored the interpretation of the immediacy of sensation. Hence, he shifted from description to expression, the importance of which he had already perceived in the great painters whom he admired: Frans Hals for his boldness, Vélasquez for his elegance. In the future, sensation would no longer necessarily be conveyed through the visual presence but through a mental leap where memory and association played an important part.

The passage from the female figure to air and water, from reality to the world of the elements, was just a small step but one which required freedom, learned and acquired, from convention.

Manet had lived too many years by the canons of painting to not be, quite naturally, tempted to merge the world in his sensations. Everything in his nature pushed him towards this step, but his culture was in conflict with his temperament. And above all, he found himself alone on this path, and opposed on all sides. He was a forerunner and young artists would go on to define this aesthetic, among others a poet named Mallarmé.

Sensation crystallized in thought was threatened with vertigo but also with sterility, Mallarmé was aware of this. All his life he strained towards this unique book, which by the manipulation of the medium (which is by definition a painting), could be embodied in the chemistry of colors. The subject was no longer but a pretext.

A pretext or alibi. Or accomplice.

It was in the name of this complicity that Manet found his pictorial orientation through female presence, while Monet, for example, found it in the landscape. An urban dweller, Manet would never know the inebriation of the self transcended by nature; a gentlemen, he would find its equivalent is women. His painting, like Mallarmé's poetry, was directly inspired by society, to make of it a pictorial poem.

Forms of reality and sensation combined in this color-laden brushstroke, destroyer of luminosity which from this time in canvas after canvas continued its valiant and generous prayer. At the time this was considered an affront, when it was merely innovation; it was seen as negligence when it foreshadowed all that art would be: an affirmation of the fundamental unity of reality and who is affected by it, expresses it, "makes it visible", no longer through the knowledge of its shortcomings and errors, which is subject to contradiction, but through sensation, which snaps its fingers at the frontiers where knowledge stops, overturns the order of cultural conventions and places creation at the center of the world, transcending the viewpoint that distributed various specific roles to painting: landscape, portrait, still life, genre scene, historical art. At the very heart of the world, the painter could listen to the great currents that coursed through it and gave it life.

Madame Manet at the Piano.

Autumn.
Nancy, Musée des Beaux-Arts.

Le Bon Bock.
Private collection.

LE BON BOCK

Monet had just finished painting Berthe Morisot in a black hat and his disturbing *Brune aux Seins Nus*, a delicate still life with a fan, scented with violets, and where Mallarmé's shadow emerges in the wings. He decided to paint an habitué of the café Guerbois: the lithographer Emile Bellot, whose rough physicality had appealed to him. This was not the first time that he had been attracted to a model for his physical qualities, but from the very start it posed a different type of pictorial approach, one which diverged from the beaten path, where the technique could not derive its energy from outside of the subject but had to remain absolutely faithful to the subject himself. Thus the subject became the pretext, the *raison d'être* for the painting, and its potential verve. This was the case with this portrait, all the moreso because ever since his return from Holland Manet had harbored a great admiration for the style of Frans Hals, at once open, rich and mocking. He was to interpret it in his own way. It took no less than twenty sittings to achieve the final result of an harmonious blend of freshness of touch, spontaneity, keenness of observation, vigor of expression and a composition that all agreed, even the most intransigeant, was a triumph. It was a great success for the painter when it was presented at the 1872 Salon. His peers, however, thought that Manet had become bogged down in tradition, that his reference was too pointedly to Frans Hals, the overall effect was too "old masterish", far from the boldness that the artist seemed to advocate in his conversations at the café Guerbois. They were not far from accusing him of opportunism.

That this work had been accepted and acclaimed by those who prohibited admission to the Salon of Manet's companions, the group of artists from Les Batignolles, proved to the latter that they had no chance of ever getting in if they remained faithful to their style. Quarrels and bad feelings. Manet accused his companions of abandoning him, although they had never even tried (apart from Renoir) the experience of the Salon, sure that it could only be a

The Folkstone at Boulogne.

Study for a beach painting.
Private collection.

On the Beach.
Private collection.

negative one and the source, for them, of renewed disappointments, bitterness and discouragement.

The idea of a special Salon, an exhibition organized and controlled by those who were to be the eternal "refusés", took hold, and the most energetic among them decided to make this dream a reality.

At Boulogne, where Manet went to relax with his family (he returned there several times) he discovered the virtues of the *plein air* technique. Whether by happy and strange coincidence, destiny or a question of logic, Manet (who was an occasional sailor) found in the sea a new dimension in painting that for him replaced his museum culture and his references to the past, a fundamental part of his work and a hindrance to his transition to the *plein air* technique which everybody around him was using. "More bizzarre than moving. His work is weak. To what is this sterility owing?" Castagnary wrote of Manet when he had presented his *Le Déjeuner* and *The Balcony* at the 1869 Salon, canvases so laboriously constructed.

By attempting a natural subject which had something of the landscape and something of the life of men (to which Manet was never insensitive) was a pure test of his talent, since the museum references to which he had confined himself (if one is to believe his detractors) were here of no use. It resulted in a succession of canvases made with a generous hand, sensitive to real details, but also capable of grasping all the music of space. *Moonlight on the Port of Boulogne*, with its eerie glimmers in a great deployment of clouds and a vigorous rhythm of sails and masts at a fantasmic speed, demonstrates Manet's stylistic freedom and his maturity in the face of new artistic requirements.

The portrait of Eva Gonzales, and especially that of Berthe Morisot in *Repose*, mark the painter's return to the private world of femininity which constitutes a sort of leit motif in his work.

But they are also the preliminary stage, no doubt necessary, to the woman in *Garden*, his first *plein air* work in the Impressionist manner – that is, taking a banal contemporary subject within the framework of its own environment: there, at the home of the painter de Nittis in Saint-Germain-en-Laye, in his with in all probability the latter's wife as his model. The air circulates freely around the figure candidly placed in space, with the face shown front on and the body slightly turned and generously enveloped in the whiteness of a dress. This whiteness was a lively element of the symphony of light that plays, shimmering and delicate, over a path, also diagonally placed, enlarging the space while delimiting it, describing the opulence of the garden which is as much a subject of the painting as the woman at peace with all the splendor of her femininity.

Had the war and the Commune not intervened, Manet was mature for a *plein air* style of painting.

He practised it taking subjects that were less in the spirit of Impressionism (which was just taking form) than history making itself before the painter's eyes. They were subjects suited to his talent, less because of a desire to bear witness to things but because painting was a part of his life and he painted what he saw.

One of these was *Le Petit Montrouge*, an urban landscape with a muddy, snow-covered street flowing through it like a disastrous flood. A black landscape, which provided an echo to his *Burial*, in which the painter depicted the Rue de l'Estrapade lying fallow, dominated by the powerful and somewhat wild Mouffetard hill and a horizon line punctuated by the domes of the Observatory, the Val-de-Grâce and the Panthéon, suggesting in the misty distance the presence of a big city. These are but sketches, as is the mocking and very freely done *View of the Exposition Universelle*, to be noted for the record.

An urban dweller, Manet returned often and willingly to the subjects offered him by the great scintillating city in all of its glorious blaze. He did not seek the epic, or grandeur, nor the controversial, but he recorded with great warmth of feeling whatever he saw.

In this, like Renoir, Monet and Pissarro, he was perfectly in harmony with his times. They were all witnesses of the great city frolicking around them as they painted the noise of the boulevards, the flavor of the open air cafés, the bistro-dance halls and other playgrounds for pleasure, where Guy de Maupassant went to gather the budding young women who ornamented his life and his works.

The discovery of the *plein air*, in conflict with the influence of the museums, had its best results with the seascapes, *On the Beach*, and landscapes with vast horizons such as *The Swallows*. The brushstroke quickened, at once firm and light, rich and savoury, a unifying element that bound in a blaze of color the figures and the elements surrounding them (air and water) in a sort of magnificent poem of painting.

This was one of the highpoints of this art that fashioned itself in tune with the world and in the innermost folds of the universe.

Starting with a simple family event (his wife and brother stretched out on the beach) he made a composition whose anecdotal restraint shifts the focus of attention to its plasticity. He was by then ready to return among his companions at the Café Guerbois, meeting them on the same ground of their pictorial experiences and achievements.

We have come to the debut of Impressionism, recognized as an organized movement in the Parisian periphery between Gennevillier and Argenteuil, along the tranquil and rustic banks of the Seine, the hymn to a summer that they said was endless.

THE ODALISKS

Is "portrait" the correct classification of Manet's 1862 painting of Jeanne Duval, Baudelaire's irritating and fateful mistress, the one who was behind his wretchedness, but whose exotic allure fascinated the poet? Does it fit in the order of representation of named and identifiable individuals: this composition in which the subject's face becomes secondary, is relegated to the realm of the inaccessible compared to the opulence of her attire, this arrogant and haughty handling of the muslin fabric, which more than dressing the figure becomes the stuff itself of the painting?

Manet distorted the usual task of the portrait, which is to pin down the personality of its subject. It seems that he had lost interest in his model, in favor of her clothing, which is transformed into a barely controlled assault of white.

It heralded an identical handling of white in *The Reading* (1868), and the sort of indolent opulence that characterized the softly reclining women that Manet continued to paint throughout his career.

Nina de Callias (1873) and *Madame Monet Seated on a Blue Couch* (1878) express respectively a questionable taste for opulence and good bourgeois behavior. Nina de Callias was one of those women who put all their energy into their public relations. They were the keystone of social and intellectual life of the 19th century, the bourgeois version of the oracles of the 18th century who received their callers seated in an armchair in the name of the dignity of their class, and in the 19th century had settled into a reclining position in the name of comfort and courtliness. Courtliness was not always absent in this free and tolerant lifestyle that betrayed gusto for life, idea exchange and love.

Nina de Callias offered a good example of this, with her Salon in Rue Chaptal, resolutely hostile to the Empire. After the period of the Commune, she felt it wise to take refuge in Switzerland until she was guaranteed impunity. Then she took up her tumultous romantic and intellectual activity in Rue des Moines, opening her salon to a turbulent group

that included Verlaine, Mallarmé, Emmanuel Chabrier, Jean Richepin, Catulle Mendès, Villiers de l'Isle Adam, Maurice Rollinat and Paul Alexis. The poet and inventer Charles Cros acting as her faithful and attentive escort, closely followed the adventure of the portrait painted by Manet in his studio, and wrote a poem to accompany the canvas. Though it did not have the tenor of Baudelaire's for Lola de Valence, it set the tone for the rapport that was to be established between painters and writers.

Sachant qu'elle est futile, et pour surprendre à l'aise
Ses poses, vous parliez des théâtres, des soirs
Joyeux, de vous, marin, stoppant près des comptoirs,
De la mer bleue et lourde attaquant la falaise.

Autour du cou, papier d'un bouquet, cette fraise,
Ce velours entourant les souples nonchaloirs,
Ces boucles sur le front, hiéroglyphes noirs,
Ces yeux dont vos récits calmaient l'ardeur mauvaise.

Ces traits, cet abandon opulent, et ces tons
(Vous en étiez, je crois, au club des Mirlitons)
Ont passé sur la toile en quelques coups de brosse.

Et la Parisienne, à regret, du sofa
Se soulevant, dit: *"C'est charmant!"* puis étouffa
Ce soupir: *"Il ne m'a pas faite assez féroce!"*

Manet's atelier was a space for reflection, of a lone man's confrontation with the terrible problem of painting, where he rethought all of its meaning, its objectives and its content. We have a description of this place of confrontation and no doubt of sentimental effusion that dates back to the solo exhibition that the painter organized there in 1876.

"Four windows, of which three are without curtains, to brighten up this museum. Facing them are the French doors by which one enters the studio. In the righthand corner, behind a park bench painted green, stand the piano, almost invisible beneath the thousand objects that cover it: paint box, paint brushes, guitar, books, carriage basket. Music alone is lacking... The mantelpiece is cluttered with faience vases and a plaster statue of Minerva, surmounted by a raven with outstretched wings, an empty bottle, etc...

"...[There is] an oak staircase leading to a small loft where the painter, who does not live there, can take his siestas. The atelier takes its light from a large bay window, similar to those that overlook the hall of the Odéon. Today, that opening has been hidden by a green curtain, behind which it would not be surprising if the painter were standing to eavesdrop on his visitors' comments."

This was the studio in which Nina de Callias posed. Heavy curtains, heaps of cushions, precious draperies, and Japanese fans hung on the wall show a great refinement, but also an atmosphere in which sensuality vied against exoticism. Here, the model's strongly pronounced personality harmonized with the decoration that the painter has emphasized by embroidering details all around her.

IMPRESSIONISM IS BORN ALONG THE WIDE BOULEVARDS

On May 1, 1874, at the home of Nadar in 35, Boulevard des Capucines, the "Société anonyme des artistes peintures, sculpteurs et graveurs" inaugurated its first exhibition uniting such artists as Zacharie Astruc, Attendu, Béliard, Boudin, Félix Braquemond, Edouard Brandon, Bureau, Cals, Cézanne, Gustave Colin, Louis Desbras, Degas, Guillaumin, Louis Latouche, Lepic, Lépine, Levert, Alfred Meyer, Auguste de Molins, Monet, Berthe Morisot, Mulot-Durivage, de Nittis, Auguste and Léon Ottin, Pissarro, Renoir, Henri Rouart, Léopold Robert and Sisley.

Claude Monet was the mainspring of the group, which was based on the corporative partnership model. Pissarro was keen on organizational questions and closer than the others to the common people. He was careful to carry out his work with political consciousness, and was the one to suggest as a model the bakers' charter. Thus, each artist was to turn over to a common fund ten percent of the proceeds of any sales. Again, it was Pissarro to propose drawing lots for the placement of the artists' works, thus avoiding eventual friction between the artists as well as eschewing the Salon's rather stupid custom based on alphabetical order. Some of the participants were worried that the exhibition would be confused with a repeat of the Salon des Refusés. To avoid this, each of the artists helped round up as many participants as possible. Degas, among others, succeeded in enlisting artists whose style, focus, pictorial ambitions, and aesthetic viewpoints had nothing to do with those of what was to be Impressionism.

In fact, while this policy of rounding up participants of all artistic bents overcame the problem of being identified as the "refusés", it also weakened the effect of any underlying message. And the excessive and latitudinarian mixing of styles and aesthetic viewpoints made the exhibition seem the product of a fringe element, despite the commitment of the artists engaged in this struggle. Thus, it was prey to the gibes of the professional critics and the public.

The former were headed up by the rather arrogant, powerful and pedantic Albert Wolff, who went down in history for his incisive formulas and definitive judgments which accompanied Impressionism from start to finish. And the hostile and mocking attitude of the public was immortalized in a few humoristic sketches that stressed its conformism, blindness and obstinate culture of acquired ideas that was never so deeply rooted in the popular humus as in the 19th century.

The exhibition was the outcome of a lengthy theoretical gestation whose fate soon merged with that of the Impressionists. It gradually identified its aesthetic standpoints and played the role of the greyhound to an avant-garde that was still not yet aware of its strength. It sensed it, or rather, sensed the need for the change that it represented. This common front had its occult leader: it was Manet.

Nonetheless, Manet was absent from the exhibition. It was 1874 and he still insisted on presenting his work at the Salon, which remained in his opinion "the battlefield par excellence", the one on which he was to test himself against his detractors. "It was", he said, "the stronghold of cliché, whose doors it was necessary to break down". Degas was offended, accusing him of "playing the solitary knight", and of being "a vain and stubborn individual".

At the Salon, which had rejected two out of the three paintings he had submitted, he presented *The Railway*. It received fairly favorable reviews, though a few reserves and some venom were cast in the artist's way, something which by then he was used to. "Monsieur Manet", declared one critic, "belongs to a school which, unable to know or perceive beauty, has created for itself a new ideal of triviality and platitude. His painting is suitable for storefronts, and his art at its best achieves the level of signmakers' or cabaret artists'".

Beneath this will to wound and to denigrate, there is a grain of truth, a suggestion of an approach that it would be well to heed, since it placed Manet on the road of modernity that Baudelaire had wished for him, Zola had attributed to him, and Mallarmé had envied him.

Mallarmé, his neighbor, could rejoice in the same view from his windows of the new, etched into the Parisian landscape and to which Manet rendered fair tribute in his painting: the railway.

From his window in Rue de Saint-Pétersbourg Manet could take in with a single glance the Pont de l'Europe and the tracks of the Saint-Lazare railroad.

He made several sketches to prepare the canvas. He wanted to do an urban landscape, a modern *plein air*. He had Victorine Meurent pose at the intersection of Rues de Rome and de Constantinople.

A familiar scene of private life set in a context that was then completely new, playing on the contrasting effect of the richness of the woman's attire, the freshness of the little girl's dress, the attention to detail in the clothing and the hairstyles and the sort of void filled with vapor, a signalling of the mechanical behind the high, severe and dominating bars that striate the painting, but also create two completely different zones, linked by the little girl lost in contemplation of this wonderful spectacle. It is similar to Alice's transposition before the looking glass, as she stood on the frontier between the visible and the unknown, an echo of herself, repeated, inverted with respect to the world familiar to her. But here she is open to and curious about a world still full of dark mystery for the other characters who are firmly anchored in the quiet of a past, as is made apparent by their style of dress.

As in *The Balcony*, Manet sets into motion here a coming and going play on the idea of the viewer viewed that multiplies the space and upsets tradition. The painting takes on a unique dimension that the public overlooked, preferring instead to focus on stupid details such as the polish of certain areas and the incompletion of others. This, too, was something that Manet had gotten used to.

Hymn to modernity, Manet's railway opened the way for an urban poetics later taken up for exploration by Monet. By following Manet's example, he too latched onto the motif of the Gare Saint-Lazare (seen from the interior). The nervous rhythm of the bars crossing the painting was a compositional innovation and laid the foundations for a geometic dynamic that was to be exploited some decades later by the artists descended of Cubism, bards of "marvelous modernity" whom Apollinaire gratified with his faith and enthusiasm. It was just a step from this time to Ferdinand Léger's achievements, another artist who was susceptible to the fascination of the railway.

In this, Manet had gotten hold of a subject that was directly borrowed from modern life.

Can the same be said of his companions who were baptised the Impressionists in the same year? At the first exhibition Cézanne showed a view of Pontoise (*La Maison du Pendu*), and his *Modern Olympia*, a direct reference to Manet, in a bizarre and contorted outburst of a restless baroque nature that describes Cézanne's first works as he fought through the torments of his complex psychological make-up. It took an extraordinary force of effort to overcome this, to arrive at a plasticity stripped of any personal fantasy. Renoir showed a dancer; Pissarro, a white frost; Sisley, an orchard. All of which are rather hackneyed subjects, even if the technique gave freshness to their interpretation. Berthe Morisot affirmed her sense of dreamy intimism in her *The Reading* (Manet's influence can again be seen here) and Claude Monet, lastly, dispensed with his attraction for modernity in a *Boulevard des Capucines*, where the crowd is treated as a field of flowers, and his famous *Impression: Rising Sun*, which against the painter's wishes set the standard for the new painting current, even though it was but a sketch.

The distance Manet set between himself and his colleagues was not just apparent in his refusal to mix with them but also in the themes that he chose to paint – this, even though he was not faithful to them; since soon after this great success, he returned to the same vicinity, in Alfred Stevens' garden to paint *The Croquet Match*, which conformed to the style, in terms of technique and subject, that was so admired by his Impressionist friends, especially Monet. Nevertheless Monet and Manet were at the opposite poles of this trend, as proven by their respective versions of *Déjeuner sur l'Herbe*. Monet's was a hymn to nature, while Manet's scandalous version was a scene of human comedy.

One can observe an astonishing dynamic in Manet's alternation between rapprochement and distance taken in relation to the artistic current that was making its way in the avant-garde of the period.

Sometimes he anticipated it; elsewhere he conforms to its limitations and reserves, as if he were bewitched by the language of the ancients, but awesomely modern in his content.

The very name given to this group of artists is misleading. An ill-wishing critic had grabbed onto a title that Monet had off-handedly given to one of his paintings just before the encounter at Nadar's home: *Impression: Rising Sun*, a canvas that is tender and mysterious, subtle and misty. This critic thought that "Impressionists" would be an amusing name for those who utilized an identical technique of atomized color to represent a sensation. Zola, on the other hand, persisted in calling "naturalist" this manner of painting, which had already made the leap to the other side of the looking glass. Far from being based on reality in its essential manifestation, Impressionism began to take its distance from the subject, even though it had been seductive (flowers, women, water and summer skies), and to become intoxicated with its own effects. Thus, Manet bespoke of a painting style of which man continued to be the ardent center, his heart beating with the anguish of who inhabits it, while Monet was already bringing on the triumphant arrival of abstraction.

Whatever the origins, antecedents, justifications, alibis of abstract painting were, Manet was not a part of them, not even in his boldest innovations. Manet's daring lay elsewhere, in the object observed as much as in the way of showing it, in the spirit that determined his choices as much as in the way of visualizing them.

Monet's only innovation was in his technique; his subject matter was unimportant: the stream flowing through his garden, the goldfish pond, the lawn where women dressed in crinoline petticoats idled, women who were bouquets of flowers under the heat of the sun. While Manet explored the pictorial garden, he did not show the best, nor the most original part of himself there.

Surprisingly, it was less in his drift toward a brighter, happier style of painting than in his doubts, his limitations, his obstinacy and the questions that he clearly set before himself that Manet demonstrated his greatness and his singularity.

Usually, the works a painter does in his lifetime move in the direction of improvement, thanks to the experience he acquires as he is making it. The apogee is usually at the end of this process. This was true for Matisse. It was not the case with Manet, whose evolution was marked by anomaly, singularity of intent, paradox. The excuse can be found in the difficult times he experienced, the hostility he encountered. The man's greatness arose from his doubts and his setbacks, even though the Impressionists hailed him, venerated him, were ready to honor him by hanging his paintings at the center of the exhibition hall, surrounded by their own paintings which owed so much to his innovations. But, absent from this exhibition hall, Manet appears to have desired only recognition by the common enemy: the official artists who feared him and had done everything to exclude him from their path of glory. This meant a paradoxical situation and frightening solitude for the painter who had eyes only for the Académie, while others awaited him anxiously at the Café Guerbois.

He was there, head held high and proud, with elegant bearing and brilliant conversation. He was listened to and admired. And yet, apart from his discourses, he did nothing, not even lend his support to a cause, to justify the prestige that he accumulated in the midst of the scorn and scandal fermenting in the minds of a public taken aback by his singularity and his experiments, whose only value lay in their surprising novelty.

But in a period in which being too novel was frowned upon, in which habit was the order of the day and anything which could disrupt it was met with fear, in which the established order was considered much more valuable than the risk of a promised order, dreamers, adventurers and innovators were badly thought of.

Manet represented neither one nor the other camp. He was so similar to those who rejected him that it all seems to have been a great misunderstanding. Perhaps the key can be found in the mysterious affair in which Zola got the better of Baudelaire, explaining why Zola spoke of naturalism when he meant Impressionism, because for him, Manet was an Impressionist, i.e. a naturalist. This, because he esteemed Manet, and understood him. And yet none of the pseudo-scientific blundering that shaped Zola's analysis can put together the pieces of the pictorial puzzle that Manet embodied.

He remains a puzzle. The pieces cannot be put together; they do not have the supposed logic of the lifework of others, whose every choice can be explained (even the weaknesses). Manet had one foot in one camp, one foot in another, and his head elsewhere.

There remains the question of how we can draw the connections between the canvases that conformed to the museum tradition (while still distorting its meaning) and those that flirted with the Impressionists' *plein air* technique and those that at times overlapped the two styles and intermingled them.

Just when he appeared to have settled on one style, here came another and yet another. This alternation is quite amazing and not at all facetious (not that Manet was utterly lacking in a sense of humor); instead it is the symptom of a quest and the sense of vertigo that accompanied it in all of his sincerity.

Manet contradicted himself in the name of this sincerity. Contradicted? A look at the succession of paintings – *Le Bon Bock* (1872) after *The Reading* (1868), *The Railway* (1877) after *On the Beach* (1873), the portrait of Desboutin (1875) after *Boating* (1874), *La Chanteuse de Café Concert* (1880) after the portrait of Clemenceau (1879) – shows that he did not work in a single direction, but zigzagged between the most fruitful, bold and self-destructive innovations and an instinctive respect for the formulas, styles, pictorial gimmicks which seemed obsolete, but by which he perhaps hoped to gain some recognition.

His career was quite unlike that of Cézanne, who worked inexorably in the direction of a progressive stripping of all that he wished to forget in order to regain the heart of the vision that he had invented (had he continued he might have arrived at the complete void of Malevich). Or that of Monet, who progressively shed layers of reality until he had reduced it to nothing (a ripple of grass on an expanse of water). Manet's art veered this way and that, as if the painter, gripped with remorse, wanted to offer the guarantee of a respectability that he regretted having lost. Unless we consider that Manet's progress was just more difficult to see than that of the others or his scruples were on a higher order than the merely social and that he had an infinitely loftier, more rigorous, and more ambitious vision of painting. He gazed at the world while reflecting on it: the expression of resources hidden to sight. Questions of social conditions and of painting are incompatible except at a level that is very difficult to reach.

Manet seemed to be driven by something irrepressible within himself that led him down various paths, but still with the awareness that to run too fast meant getting lost.

An adventurer against his will, this was no doubt because he never wanted to admit that he had "fallen" to the level of the Impressionists, that he shared similarities with them. He placed painting at a very high level that was based on a handling of the medium that reflected established tradition – a tradition the existence and value of which the Impressionists denied.

Manet was not for breaking with the past, but rather upheld its continuity. For him, the museum tradition counted, and he turned to it over and over again, copying the "masters" of the past, as if to wrest some deeply hidden secret from them.

"The water isn't that color! Oh, *pardon*, it is at times, as when it is green and gray, or at others when it has buff and slate-colored reflections", observed J. K. Huysmans. He was well-versed in matters of water. He had been the explorer of the Bièvre, following, driven by despair and lucidity, the meandering course of this unfortunate river ruined by industry, a river so ugly that it was kept well-hidden from sight. It had been murdered.

In Paris, already there was no more water that was in harmony with the whims of the sky. One had to leave the city and seek it in rustic spots where innocent maidens flocked on Sundays away from the frowns of the big city to go boating with their strapping young companions. These were the people that Maupassant described with a truth that shocked those of finer sensiblities. And they were the subject of Manet's *Boating*, painted in Gennevilliers, opposite what was then the large suburb of Argenteuil, where Caillebotte lived. The latter is famous especially for the collection that brought Impressionism to the Louvre, and he was an avid boater as well as amateur painter, and not an insignificant one at that.

Monet settled there in a lovely house that he painted. Renoir visited the place often. Manet spent his Sundays, and once an entire summer, there. He observed Monet painting, and adopted his light and lively, immediate style which brought to the canvas all the vibrancy of light in space.

Hostile to pure landscape, however, Manet also filled this natural space with all the figures of his entourage.

The result was a series of compositions where the river, the garden, the grassy banks were the altars of repose where ordinary men and women could live simply and for the moment. One, proud of his nonchalance at the helm of a large boat, the other simply gracious (it was Madame Monet) in the blaze of a garden's colors. The attention to the truth of the moment led Manet to paint this astonishing portrait of Monet at work, entitled *Monet in His Bateau-*

Atelier. It is a variation on the voyeur caught in flagrante delicto, here protected by the complicity of artists living the same adventure, brothers in the practice of their art.

Argenteuil was the slightly delayed echo of what had been the meeting place of "la Grenouillère" in 1869, where Monet and Renoir worked side by side on the same motifs, of which water took the precedence, as they discovered its fascinating responsiveness to subtle and rapid changes in light.

To capture the effect of water's reverberations and reflections, the brushstrokes had to become more fragmented.

Monet's awareness of the acquatic phenomenon as a subject for painting launched him onto the terrain of a watery reverie that, anticipating Gaston Bachelard, had the substance of true psychoanalysis.

In Argenteuil, Monet rediscovered the fertile water of reverie, and Manet discovered it, along with the difference between fresh and ocean water, having already depicted the latter in his seascapes and harborviews.

The harbor: a group of boats with the water merely as a support; in Argenteuil the water was not only a support but also a vibrant, alive medium whose transparency and fluidity Manet did an admirable job of conveying. While painting the people who were familiar with it and gave themselves over to its pleasures, Manet also was skilled at painting the water's liquidity.

While painting the portraits of his friends who posed unaffectedly for him in the calm and sweet flow of everyday activities, it was only natural that Manet should also paint a portrait of the water, in all of the versions that its delicate sensitivity created, just as Huysmans had described it.

NANA AND HER SISTERS

Zola did not invent Nana. She was for him the reflection of an epoch. Its product. A residue, scintillating and dazzling, but condemned to the disgrace of a society that wallowed in affluence and indecency. Historians all agree that the Second Empire in its final stage was almost Babylonian, where high society set the example for moral laxity and lust.

This led to a backlash of prudishness when the Third Republic found it necessary to impose a program for the reform of a society that had gone into collapse with the fall of the Empire and the brief blaze-up of the Commune.

One a consequence of the other, the pendulum of History swung to its extremes, and art eternalized them in stereotypes.

Nana was one of these stereotypes, a favorite of both Zola and Manet, and though their versions were similar, they were not identical.

Zola's Nana was animal-like and would have suited Degas' world of young things who were more wildcats than kittens. She embodied a society that was courting its own ruin, carrying the objects of her seduction down with her in her degeneracy. Manet's Nana was less marked by such a harsh and troubling destiny; the painter did not wish for her that character of bewitching fatality.

And yet, the true life models for these two Nanas were more or less the same.

One of these was a demimondaine whom Manet had met at the Tortoni café, where they were both habitués. The mistress of the Prince of Orange, she was known as "Citron" (Lemon), a name which suited her to perfection. She was a vestige of the sexual splendor of the Second Empire which had been dominated by the insolent, irritating and flashy figure cut by Grammont-Carderouse. Like most of her colleagues, she had tried her hand at theatre. An alibi, theatre often served as the springboard to wanton careers.

Her talent as an actress was mediocre, and she appeared only in productions which were very quickly forgotten. Her stage career having gone up in smoke she turned to setting hearts on fire. The Citron who posed for Manet, however, was already in her decline, a bit faded or on the way to being so. She was sweeter and more benevolent thanks to the wisdom acquired in the wake of too many mad adventures. This seemed to save her from a serious physical and spiritual decay.

Her real name was Henriette Hauser, and the canvas was entitled *La Toilette*. It brought to Manet yet another scandalous success. J.K. Huysmans saw in it the foreshadowing of Zola's *Nana*, which was just being published in installments, having reached the point where Nana was still a brazen little urchin, gradually being transformed into a terrible and cruel adventuress.

Zola's models were Blanche d'Antigny and Valtesse de la Bigne (whose portrait Manet would also do) in a heavy atmosphere of rented beds, provocative lingerie and shameful eroticism. They were "the pets". Low-born, her noble-sounding name an invention, having made her fortune but always avid for more, Valtesse de la Bigne is a prime example of those who settled in 96 Boulevard Malesherbes, in the heart of the Monceau plain. This was the fiefdom of the trollops and celebrated official artists who intermingled so promiscuously that it began to be called the "artists' union". Her official lover was Gervex, reknown for his role in the overly-acclaimed *Rolla*, a light comedy that put well in evidence the dominant character of an epoch that would find its Shakespeare in Labiche, its Molière in Feydeau and its Mozart in Offenbach.

Huysmans saw a version of Nana in Manet's work, "with her complicated and knowing perversity, her extravagance and her rich bawdiness. She does not detract from this gallery of loose women with which he peopled this racy Paris, sensual, somewhat degraded and flamboyant, that he has described in paintings ranging from *The Barmaid* to *Chez le Père Lathuille*, and whose culmination lies in an almost symphonic representation of all the vices of this period, *Bar at the Folies-Bergères*".

Meanwhile, in keeping with Manet's established pattern of subjects approached and repudiated, he had been stalking other models in diverse milieus, mainly his own (where elegance could mask even the naughtiest behavior).

The Skating Rink was an establishment in Rue Blanche where one could mix with a light-hearted and sporting crowd, drunk with the spinning motion, the light, colors and noise of the place. Also the sensations. The spectacle was provided by those who went there. Actors and spectators made up a game of alternation that was a constant factor in Manet, whose favorite subject for his painting was the spectacle, ostentation and exhibitionism of high society.

An habitué of the cafés, like Degas and many of his contemporaries, Manet offered compositions that captured their lively tone, the crackling of the fires of intertwining lights and scintillating reflections that highlight the customer. He did a number of portraits of his friends in this setting, in the hustle-bustle of the barmaids brazenly brandishing their beer in the midst of the crowd. From *La Serveuse des Bocks* to *Le Café*, it is one long hymn of praise to public life. A vigorous and turbulent life conveyed with quick, incisive brushstrokes to capture reeling shapes and lights which flatten out and interpenetrate, sculpting the space with their insistence and vivacity.

Au Café, like *La Serveuse des Bocks* depicted the Cabaret de Reichshoffen, Boulevard de Rochechouart. It was one of Manet's favorite places, where he handled with nonchalance slices of life that were representative of the spirit of modernity. In these paintings he finally achieved a style of painting that was perfectly suited to the theme that he had chosen.

It was a style that we might say was directly related to the special quality of the time, place and event that was unfolding before the painter's eyes. In this it was consistent with his vision, but not at all headed for abstraction. While Manet's technique

A Paris Café.

and style were modern, they did not contribute to a painting that rejected reality, but rather contributed to reality, thanks to his painting.

This is the reason why *The Bar at the Folies-Bergères* is a pure masterpiece.

BISTROS, DANCE HALLS AND CO.

Before the Café Guerbois became the headquarters of those who were preparing the new style of painting, the Café de Bade (26 Boulevard des Italiens) was Manet's preferred haunt. Every evening he went there at about five o'clock, when natural light failing, he was forced to abandon his studio. He was viewed as a person of depth and intelligence, of influence. His words and topics of discussion attracted attention. He was an opinion leader and people adopted his points of view and ways of thinking.

Behind the elegance at times heavy with pride, he was a deeply generous man of heart and soul.

Zola described him as being of "medium height, not tall, with blond hair and a slightly flushed face, a lively and intelligent gaze; his mouth was expressive, and at times mocking, his face as a whole irregular and animated, with an indescribable expression of sensitivity and energy".

His mildness, attested to by Zola and others, was more a product of his breeding than his temperament, which was rather quick. And quick to anger. And outbursts.

Witnesses stress that he tended to be "ironic in his conversation, and often cruel". Not as ruthless as Degas, but rather comfortable with shock tactics.

They were both to be found at the Café Guerbois (11 Grand Rue des Batignolles, later 19 Avenue de Clichy) in a district that was still rustic, the Montmartre hill, minus the Sacre Coeur, was to the east and to the west sloping down gently were a series of farms, vineyards and fields. The last signs of a natural life that was soon to be engulfed by the growing city.

Guerbois, like Pére Lathuille's tavern (7 Avenue de Clichy), was typical of those establishments that grew up on the shifting outskirts of town, on a sort of no man's land between city and countryside that was favorable to the explosion of pleasure spots. In the 18th century there were the Folies, in the 19th a succession of taverns, pothouses, dancehalls and cafés with liberal customs and picturesque clientele.

The Guerbois was the sounding board for the new ideas that were leading up to Impressionism. From 1876 on, the success of Impressionism confirmed by the scandal it had stirred, the small group of friends that had formed around the Café Guerbois moved to the "Nouvelle Athènes", near Place Pigalle. Degas had something to do with this, having found that it was nearer to his home at 15 Rue Laval. So, there they were in the fiefdom of the "clichyens", the name given to the artists of Boulevard de Clichy.

Veyrassat lived at number 7, Diaz at 11, Sarah Bernhard at 36, Alfred Stevens had a garden apartment at the corner of the Boulevard and Rue des Martyrs, and Victorine Meurent, who had also taken up painting, lived at number 1 of the Boulevard.

The live-wire of the Nouvelle Athènes group was Marcelin Desboutin. Monet has left a portrait of him in which he tried to convey the eccentric character of this bohemian and strange personnage who had rubbed shoulders with the Impressionists and even exhibited with them in 1876. He was a legendary figure, rumored to be a fabulously rich prince driven to ruin by his wild lifestyle.

Another habitué of the Nouvelle Athènes was a young Britisher, George Moore, who left to posterity more anecdotes than substance, but whose elegant and fashionable profile must have conquered Manet, who made a sketch of him.

On his part, Moore left an interesting description of Manet, stressing the fineness of his features, a jutting chin framed by a handsome blond beard, an aquiline nose, very pale grey eyes, a pleasantly resonant voice, his physical poise underlined by a very careful elegance, which though unaffected was exaggerated.

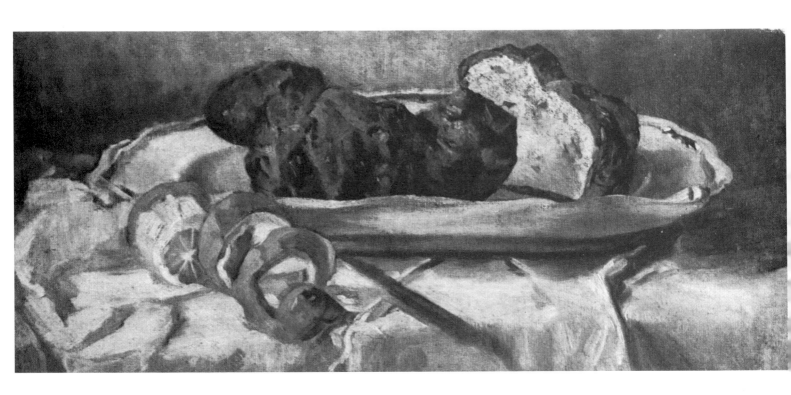

WORDS AS ARMS – MANET AND THE WRITERS

People protested on all sides, in all places, at all times. If there ever was a period of deep-set unrest, it was the 19th century, sparks afly and frightened, but stifled by the order imposed from on high. In the lower ranks, however, behind the scenes, in a subterranean realm, doubt wrought havoc and protest stirred in peoples' minds.

In the 18th century this was the prerogative of the rich; in the 19th century it was that of the forgotten.

The forgotten were those overlooked by the bourgeoisie, the same who had silenced Monsieur Thiers, crushed the Commune and imposed its own moral dictatorship. Theirs was an omnipresent power that prohibited any deviation. And yet, doubts grew in the face of this regime which hid the essential truth of things, people and their lives.

Far from being the devastating, thundering outburst that it was in 1789, penetrating to the king's inner chambers, protest now smouldered under the embers. Its effects were delayed and its projects were postponed.

By dint of postponement, its road was strewn with martyrs, those who had given themselves body and soul to this adventure of the mind – not just for strayed intellectuals, but a widespread raising of consciousness. The proof is that the enlightened bourgeois joined on the battleground the laborer who had been stripped, robbed of the rights he had won in 1789. The agitators were the artists and the writers, who set the example, and so doing became legendary.

It is significant that scenes of History which had always been occupied by the figures holding the power were now occupied by men who did not have any at all. Until this time history had been confused with those who made it. Now, it was made in an occult way, by those who challenged its course, its management by functionaries who hid behind their institutions.

History was being made behind the scenes.

The close of the 19th century was a great breeding ground for genius and revolt, from Lautréamont to

Rimbaud, Gauguin to van Gogh. A fragile thread was held out, on which we hung all our hopes and dreams, our desires.

We can only imagine what our intellectual, spiritual and moral future would have been without these men of fiery hearts, mild eyes, and bold action who dreamed, drew, described, presented and invented the world as we want it today.

Innovation played a key role in this. And because innovation is an arm, it often turned back against those who used it. In Manet's case, this innovation was not conspicuous, because he was not equipped to make use of it.

His course is all the more fascinating for the opposition he came up against in his milieu and in himself.

Those who profited by his example were firm in their convictions. He was beset by doubts, misunderstood on all sides, by those whom he repudiated and those whom he wanted to join, In him, there was none of van Gogh's pathologically suicidal commitment, obsessed with himself, with his own destiny, with the fires that gnawed at him from within. Nor did he have any of Cézanne's determined quest for austerity of form that in the end led to his complete alienation from those who were close to him. And the Impressionists, were they not the continuers of a style of painting that was in serene physical and mental harmony with its surroundings? They were driven to the extreme limits of a plastic language and its possibilities for expression, in the logic of a predictable progression. For Manet, the struggle was step by step, harsh, impassioned and though always controversial, propped up by the support he needed and received from Baudelaire, Zola and Mallarmé – hence the importance of their contribution.

BAR AT THE FOLIES-BERGERES

It had taken its name from the Rue Bergère. It was one of those places for amusement and shows that were so popular at the end of the last century. Half honky-tonk, half cabaret whose gallery was a meeting ground for the most colorful and diverse crowd.

It was the Opéra at a popular level.

The Folies-Bergères gallery was a mecca for fashionable society. Manet, like many of his friends, loved to go there, where even high society matrons did not disdain making their appearances. During the intermissions the foyer was the site of a social parade, with a tawdry side too, that rivalled that of theaters with much more ambitious aims than its own, even if theater in this period was less of an intellectual exercise than a social pretext for a night out, and assuredly not a refined expression of a literary form.

In choosing the Folies-Bergères as his subject, Manet settled a score with public opinion. His aim in this masterful painting was twofold, but not contradictory: to carry out a superb example of painting technique and to bear witness to the modernity conveyed by this space, closed yet at the same time scintillating, spiritual, sensual and through the effect of the mirror, many-layered and injected with energy.

In fact, the quality of the painting technique did not detract from its subject; indeed, it exalted it. The subject in turn, despite its appeal, did not overshadow the impact of the pictorial handling.

It suffices to look at a few of the details to realize this. In particular, the line-up of glassware and bottles shows how he captured the transparency of the objects with a quick brushstroke, reduced to the essential, though also sensual. At once sensitive to the materiality that it exalts and to the play of light, this painting is a "pictorial machine" that functions simultaneously as a still life (the foreground), a portrait (of the barmaid) and an overview – this shimmering of figures reflecting in the mirror, some of which are identifiable. Mery Laurent is recognizable (in white), and Ellen Andrée (wearing a cape),

Bar at the Folies-Bergères.
London, Courtauld Institute.

whom Degas had already had pose for his disturbing painting *Absinthe*. A professional model before acting in Antoine's troupe, she appeared in many of Manet's compositions, including *The Parisian Woman* (1874), *Au Café* (1878), the portrait *Young Woman on the Bench* (1878), and Manet had planned to include her in his *Chez le Père Lathuille*, but since she did not show up as he was concluding the sitting, he substituted her with a professional model.

Mery Laurent was a close friend of Mallarmé, who introduced her to Manet, and a loyal friendship blossomed between the two. She was a theater-person who rose to fame as a scantily-clad performer. An astonished audience had discovered her in *La Belle Hélène*, when she was just seventeen. "Kept" by a rich American, she enjoyed receiving artists in her apartment in Rue de Rome and in her "field house". This was the "villa des Talus", at, Boulevard Lannes, which overlooked the fortification ditches, and hence its name.

Manet did a portrait of her which inspired Mallarmé to write his famous postal quatrains:

> "A Mademoiselle Mery
> 'Laurent qui vit loin des Profanes
> 'en sa maison very
> 'select du neuf boulevard Lannes."

In 1894 (Manet had already died) Mery Laurent moved from this modest house to a very particular pseudo-Renaissance residence. Mallarmé, Henri Becque, Catulle Mendès, J.K. Huysmans often visited, along with François Coppée, who honored his hostess with another quatraine:

> Mery j'ai pour ton nouveau gîte
> fait un ciment à ma façon
> et mon voeu le plus tendre habit
> chaque pièce de ta maison."

Mallarmé completed it with:
> Ouverte au rire qui l'arrose

> telle, sans que rien d'amer y
> séjourn, une embaumante rose
> du jardin royal de Mery.

Of Manet's female models, Mery was the one whose features he seemed most to enjoy immortalizing. In the year 1883 he did no less than seven portraits of her in pastel, and there is also a lovely *Autumn* of 1881.

She died in 1900, having bequeathed to Victor Margueritte, one of her last friends, a panel of *The Execution of Maximilian*, which Manet had given her.

While working on *Bar at the Folies-Bergéres*, in the fall of 1881, perhaps to play with the chromatic possibilities he had become extraordinarily skilled at, Manet did a number of portraits.

In addition to Mery Laurent, an extravagant character like so many of the period, he had others pose for him in the studio: the Countess Albazi, Madame Jules Guillemet, whose portrait he had already done in *The Greenhouse*, a flashy Irma Brummer as well as Madeleine Lemaire's little girl (the mother's salon in Rue Monceau attracted the youthful Marcel Proust in search of character models for *Le Recherche du Temps Perdu*. It was there that he found Charles Ephrussi, his model for Swann. Ephrussi was the one who arranged the meeting that led to the portrait). Manet, *salonard*, on the fringe of modern painting got his revenge painting portrait after portrait, not without a touch of self-indulgence. Had he not confessed to Carolus Duran, when he was experiencing the worst moments of his struggle for recognition and when he was the prey of the critics and the gibes of a public that had not followed his evolution, that he envied his colleague's dazzling and easy career?

In spite of its innovations, *Bar at the Folies-Bergères* was celebrated by the public and the critics at the time of its presentation at the Salon.

Nevertheless his innovation did invite a few last digs. At times a grain of truth emerges from spite:

Ernest Cheneau seemed to be shocked by Manet's composition, especially by the barmaid, and his remark is strangely salient: "It is not allowed to be more female than that creature set behind the bar".

The model, Suzon, in fact worked as the establishment's barmaid. With her "bangs" and pendant on its black cord, her heavy gaze, that sort of studied vulgarity that Manet intentionally put into her posture, represents the same type of "sweet young thing" that inspired fin-de-siècle art, especially in the Impressionist circles since they were the witnesses of their times.

This type would appear in Degas' art, but with a more declared bestiality, and in Toulouse-Lautrec's art, captured in the ambiguity of a drawing that tended towards expressionism and caricature.

Manet's version was more shocking – it was disturbing in its more precise rendering of reality. His contemporaries could hardly bear it, as if this superbly done celebration of night hid a judgment of a society as it passed before the mirror.

Garden with Shed at Bellevue.
Private collection.

Manet's Tomb. Passy Cemetery.

"Having set out to make some sketches in the park designed by Le Nôtre, I had to settle with just painting my garden. The most ghastly of gardens", wrote Manet to Eva Gonzales on September 25, 1881, giving an exact measure of his ambitions and his daily reality.

Increasingly debilitated by an illness that was to be fatal, Manet was reduced to roaming from garden to garden, which were not always at the height of his expectations. He went to Bellevue, a villa close by his friend Emilia Ambre's, in Route des Gardes, and then to Versailles (20 Avenue de Villeneuve l'Etang) and finally to Rueil, which was no better. Having failed to paint the immensity of a park – his drawings left him unsatisfied, such was the conflict between his ostentatious austerity and his painting style and the subjects he chose – he was reduced to painting the reduction of nature that he found in various gardens in various places.

Here or there, twenty paces of illusory decoration, not even the world in miniature, but a sampler of the petite bourgeois conception of nature: neatly raked paths, small lawns, arbors and pretentious clumps of flowers. It was a mediocre version of nature from which his painting genius allowed him to extract some savory bits of pure painting, a painting style that advocated Impressionism. *The Rueil House* marked a register that was unusual in Manet, on the order of pure landscape. No human presence to push the landscape back into the simple role of decoration, it highlights the instant with its dancing light modeled skilfully by the vegetation, a moment of expectation, of silence and of life, tersely evoked by the open windows of a house that must be opulent, where Manet lingered while painting "still lifes", gems of pure painting whose power he no doubt sensed. Without this, how can we explain the banality of the subject, even its poverty?

Unlike the pictorial tradition that went back as far as the beginnings of history, Manet did not amass clever compositions for the delight of painting; he did not express in his work the richness of

Breakfast in the Office.
Munich, Neue Pinakothek.

nature or some happy dreamy dimension of reality.

It is nothing but a record reduced to a very few things and tending oddly to a certain geometric precision. His pieces of fruit and flowers are less the exaltation of nature than a form captured in the painting medium, springing from its mass, its thickness, participating in a pictorial substance which seeks its order just as it is being applied.

A masterful example of this is the most essential still life in the history of this art: *Still Life with Asparagus*, where the gesture itself of painting, the thickly applied brushstroke, gives birth to the asparagus, like the supreme sign of a pictorial action that finds there self-justification.

Manet's boldness – so censured by the critics, so badly received when it treated subjects reflecting a too-frankly declared reality, perceived as an improper declaration at a time when it was not good to speak the truth – found in the still life a terrain without obstacles. This, because it was stripped of all social connotations when taken for what it was not: a simple observation of nature. But it was not just this, because going beyond his usual voyeurism, Manet started to direct his gaze elsewhere: on the paint itself.

In the 19th century, courtly painting had used up its resources. Cornered, those who refused to entertain the illusion of its revival, which they knew was impossible, had no other recourse but to treat painting no longer as the terrain of pomposity, but as the terrain of confidences, whispers, confession, questions.

Nothing comes of provocation, if not a bad view of what is disturbing, for its novelty as well as because this style of painting, so simple in its aims, so obvious in its ambitions, broke a habit as old as art, and which had ensured the prestige of art, eventually creating confusion between the two.

Painting of the 19th century took its scandalous character from its different aims, its naturalness, the intimate rapport with life that it implied (including that of the artist himself).

Having been one of the first to note this difference, to have sensed it and to have desired to experiment with it, Manet was to be the most criticized.

He refused to play the game; he did not sing the hymn to grandeur broadcast by the School, the pedantic Académie. He was sincere with himself and was keenly aware of the new rapport the artist had to have with reality, instead of serving who was in power.

In the hands of the bourgeoisie, art had recovered in theatricality what it had lost in essentiality, and it found in grandiloquence what it had lost in depth. There were neither gods nor kings to sustain it, just the ordinary. Gazes that were accustomed to the lives of the gods and goddesses, and of the martyrs, now had only the platitudes dished up over and over again by painters who looked no further than the ends of their noses.

That painting had lost its grandeur was good reason to be upset for whoever demanded to be transported and moved by art. That it had been emptied of all meaning became a provocation, a reason for the anger that *Olympia* aroused, for example.

The painting appeared scandalous because Manet put no intentions into it. Not even that of the eroticism that the bourgeois, so smitten with painted morality, had no qualms about identifying between the lines of a well-trussed anecdote.

Vulgarity was not far from sickly sentimentality and preciousness. *Olympia* was neither sublime nor vulgar. She was a disturbing absence that bore the appearance of presence. Manet had not prettified the nudity that he painted, because he painted it from a position of neutrality before a subject that perhaps interested him less than the pictorial technique he used to highlight the color areas and textures. The flesh, the flowers, the fabrics, the shadow, the cat are examples of pure painting, effects achieved with the medium. Moreover, they have a touch of mystery which necessarily arises from the quality of painting, whatever the subject; it is the artist's spirit, his dreams, which show through any subject, but especially through what is stated clearly, as if the unconscious is best expressed through the unsaid, the sensed, than through the anecdote which imprisons, stiffens the discourse.

There are no striking details in Manet's life, none of the ingredients that lend themselves to legend. Well-born, living in harmony with an epoch that favored pleasure, he experienced it fully and without shame, and said it outloud whenever those around him denounced him. This led to his being misunderstood. He died in his bed. And like Rimbaud, he had had a limb amputated.

His body mutilated: we are not sure now that he was aware of this. It was as if he had been swept away by the sleep of death, bonvivant, the jolly companion, the eternally youthful lover. He let himself be swept away in the lethargy of eternal sleep, without outburst, without cries, without all the theatrics that usually accompany the great and terrible deaths of poets, just as legend would have it.

He was struck down by death, but with a sort of serenity that accompanies men without shadows, when the incomplete work has much more to teach than this bourgeois banality which might have led him down the road of conformity; he met the challenge defying conformity, just as he had demanded something different from what painting had offered until he appeared. He made it into something alive, material, warm, passionate. The stuff of delight. But not only: the breadth of a question renewed from subject to subject without there being any point in common except that which leaves us with uncertainty before his works with regard to content. Uncertain of the conclusions that could be drawn from them, of the interpretation that it should be given.

A serene and transparent life, works that are full of commotion and shadow.

But there is no doubt that the shadow cast by his works is today what most fascinates us about him.

1832	Edouard Manet is born on January 23 in Paris, son of Auguste, Personnel Manager at the Ministry of Justice. His mother is the daughter of a diplomat in Stockholm.
1839-45	Manet attends school at Vaugirard, later he enters Rollin College where he meets Antonin Proust who will become his close friend for life.
1848	He decides to become a navy officer but is rejected and he signs on as junior pilot on a merchant ship.
1849	He again fails the entrance examination for navy officer. His father accepts his decision to be a painter.
1850	In January he attends Couture's atelier, where he will regularly attend for six years.
1853	Travels to Italy, particularly fascinated by Florence.
1856	Leaves Couture's atelier and moves to a new one in Rue Lavoisier. Travel to Holland, Germany and Italy.
1858	Paints "Buveur d'Absinthe". Couture is strongly critical and their friendship comes to an end.
1859-60	At the Louvre he meets Berthe and Edma Morisot, talented painters. Paints *Musiques aux Tuileries* which is very successful among his friends, Baudelaire in particular.

1861	The Salon accepts the *Spanish Guitar Player* and Manet receives *honorable mention.*
1862	His father dies and Manet inherits a considerable fortune but is unable to administer it properly. Meets Victorine-Louise Meurent who agrees to become the model for some of his most famous paintings.
1863	Marries Suzanne Leenhoff in Holland. Send some of his works to the Salon, including *Déjeuner sur l'Herbe*, but all are rejected. Meets Nadar the photographer and the painters de Nittis, Degas, Monet and Pissarro.
1864	At last the Salon accepts two of his paintings *Corrida* and *Dead Christ and Two Angels.*
1865	His painting *Olympia* at the Salon raises scandal. Nine of his paintings are exhibited at the Galerie Martinet. Travels to Spain where he meets Théodore Duret.
1866	Meets Zola. Decides to exhibit his paintings in his studio.
1867	Manet's paintings are not accepted in the Exposition Universelle. Baudelaire dies. Manet paints Zola's portrait.

1868	In the summer at Boulogne-sur-Mer Manet gets inspiration to paint *Breakfast in the Studio*.
1869	Meets a young woman painter, Eva Gonzales: she will be his only pupil.
1870	Manet has a duel with the art critic Duranty who is slightly wounded. Manet is drafted as an officer when the war between France and Prussia breaks out.
1871	Returns to Paris with his family during the insurrection. He is elected to the Artist Guild of La Commune. Fighting in the streets inspires engraving of *Civil War*.
1872	Shows some work at London exhibition organized by Society of French Artists. Travel to Holland with his wife.
1873	Exhibits successfully at the Salon. Fire destroys the Opéra and Manet makes sketches. Famous singer Faure buys some of his paintings.
1874	On April 15 the famous Impressionists' exhibition opens in Nadar's studio. Manet is invited but refuses to participate, considering the Salon the only appropriate place for an artist.

1875	Travels to Venice.
1876	First symptoms of his sickness start in his left foot.
1877	Work on his first naturalist painting *Nana*.
1878	His sickness progresses and he spends some time with his wife at Bellevue for treatment.
1880	Manet exhibits 25 paintings at the "Vie Moderne" attracting many visitors. Spends three months at Bellevue for treatment. Back in Paris, starts painting portraits.
1881	Rents a villa at Versailles where he moves with his family. His health gets worse. He is nominated Kinght of the "Légion d'Honneur".
1883	He cannot walk to his studio anymore. On April 6 he is confined permanently to bed. Surrounded by his closest friends, Manet dies on April 30. On May 3 the funeral takes place and Proust presents the eulogy.